PHOTOSHOP AND 3D

BRIAN TAYLOR
DAVE SMITH
NATHAN FLOOD
TOM MULLER

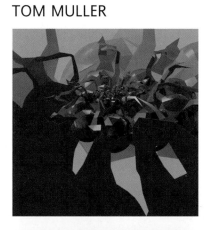

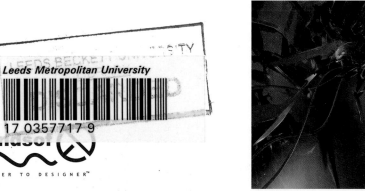
friends of ED
DESIGNER TO DESIGNER™

PHOTOSHOP AND 3D
GEOMETRY AND CHAOS

4X4 GEOMETRY & CHAOS

© 2001 friends of ED

Trademark Acknowledgements

friends of ED has endeavored to provide trademark information about all the companies and products mentioned in this book by the appropriate use of capitals. However, friends of ED cannot guarantee the accuracy of this information.

First printed October 2001

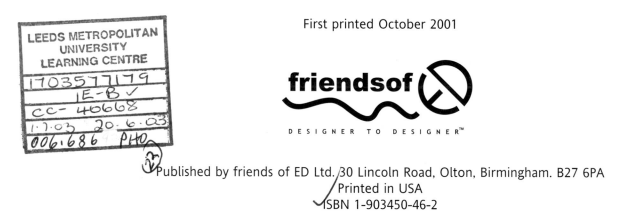

friendsof
DESIGNER TO DESIGNER™

Published by friends of ED Ltd. 30 Lincoln Road, Olton, Birmingham. B27 6PA
Printed in USA
ISBN 1-903450-46-2

4X4 GEOMETRY & CHAOS

PHOTOSHOP AND 3D

credits

authors
brian taylor
dave smith
nathan flood
tom muller

author agent
mel jehs

project administrator
thomas stiff

copyright research
thomas stiff

team leader
joanna farmer

technical assistance
peter aylward

creative consultant
brian taylor

cd
tom bartlett

content architect
catherine o'flynn

lead editor
jon hill

editor
paul thewlis

graphic editor
deb murray

technical reviewers
chris dewey
corné van dooren
andrés yáñez durán
deb murray
todd simon
jon steer

proof readers
joanna farmer
mel jehs

index
simon collins
emily colborne

BRIAN TAYLOR: 11

DAVE SMITH: 65

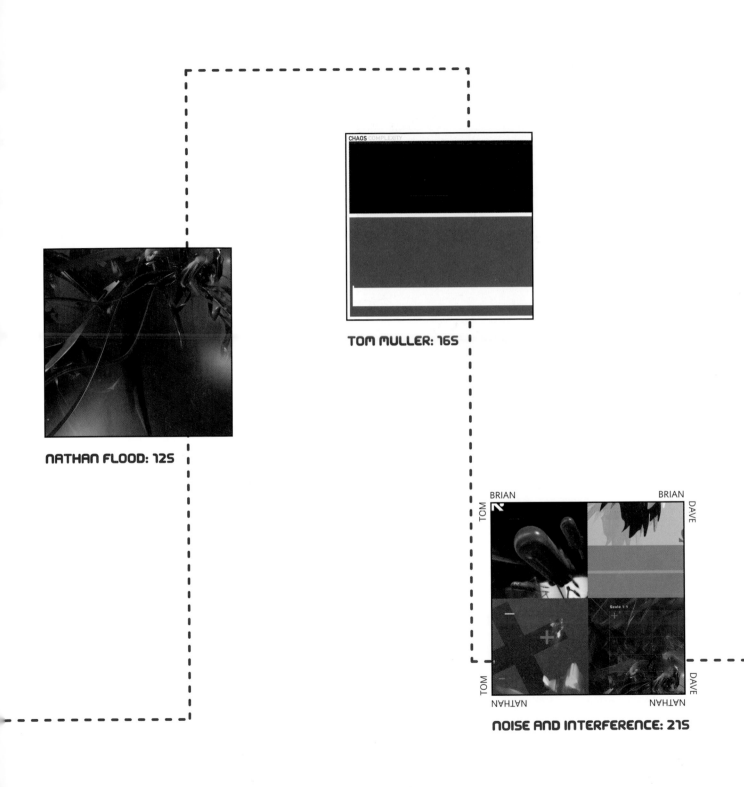

NATHAN FLOOD: 12S

CHAOS COMPLEXITY

TOM MULLER: 16S

BRIAN   BRIAN
TOM   DAVE

TOM   DAVE
NATHAN   NATHAN

NOISE AND INTERFERENCE: 21S

BRIAN TAYLOR
Brian Taylor works from home in Dundee, Scotland. He has worked in many areas of design over the years, including graphic design, illustration (traditional and digital), multimedia, computer game design, and part-time lecturing at art college. He won first prize in the multimedia CD-ROM category at the Scottish Design Awards 1999 and was commended for the Drum Grand Prix prize. He also pursues his own personal work, including his short films (with their accompanying web site www.rustboy.com) and his portfolio site (www.XL5design.com). He is currently producing concept work for a television production company in the UK.

DAVE SMITH
Dave Smith is a Canadian digital designer working out of Vancouver BC. Before founding the design studio Math, Dave served as a freelance senior web communications designer at firms such as eyeplay communications and TribalDDB. He has produced several personal works for display online at Deepseat.net.

NATHAN FLOOD

Nathan found that a latent interest in art could be expressed in a digital form, and began working on the Web as a creative designer. He began as a junior designer at Razorfish, Inc. in New York, became a junior artist at Vir2L Technology in DC, and then a designer at The WDDG in New York. He is currently a freelance art director.

Related links:

http://nginco.com
http://www.threeoh.com
http://www.wddg.com
http://www.vir2l.com
http://www.razorfish.com

TOM MULLER

Tom was born on January 9th 1974 in Antwerp, Belgium. Early on, he was already drawing comics – and was determined to become a comic book artist. While in high school however his interests turned towards graphics and design. This set the stage for his college years: he went on to the Royal Academy for Fine Arts to study industrial design. After two years he couldn't take the scientific side any more and switched over to graphic and advertising design, where he hooked up with Steven (aka Stoav) with whom he still collaborates today.

Having seen the possibilities of the Web, he started working at Vintage after he graduated, where he worked for clients such as Ricoh, Honeywell, Johnson & Johnson, and Alpine. After 2 years he moved to London to work for the European division of Vir2L – where he worked for one year.

Aside from company-related work, he maintains his personal site ximeralabs.com, where he experiments with different approaches towards graphics and form. If he's not designing, he is either reading comics or eating sushi. And if he is designing, he listens to loud music, drinking way too much coffee and smoking a lot.

tomm@ximeralabs.com

The 4

The creative process is not a clinical or remote affair. By stepping into this project with Tom, Nathan, Dave, and Brian, you need to be prepared to get your hands dirty. This is a rocky road with highs and lows. The snags and frustrations are not airbrushed out. They will drag you through every dead end, every frustration, en route to their final vision. But from finished artwork through to remixing and cross-pollinating, you will also experience the intense buzz and excitement of creation, innovation, and collaboration. You share in the thrill of four innovative artists doing what they do best, with peers they respect and admire.

The 4x4

Most books are fossils. Designers look back on their body of work; they discuss pieces they once created in response to motivations they once had. We sit on the outside and gaze in at the pinned exhibits.

This book is not a spectator and it is not a museum piece. The 4x4 Project is a catalyst and the authors' words, the readers' thoughts, the artworks and the theories are all ongoing reactions in the creative process.

This book is a laboratory where you can learn from and participate in experimentation.

The accompanying CD provides you with relevant source files for the tutorials, the final, exclusive artworks in unflattened PSD format, and all remixes and digital hybrids spawned by the Project... the next step is yours.

enter the 4x4 project

phase 1 - the book in your hand
phase 2 - the experiment continues online

you have the theme
you have the source files
respond
react
create
combine

file-swop with other readers
create hybrids with the artists' works
share inspirations
innovate, experiment

www.friendsofed.com/4x4

I worked for years in traditional design, in the days when 'cut and paste' required scalpels and cow-gum, but even then I had a fascination with the 3D computer graphics in films like Tron, and the early Pixar shorts. It took a few years before computers capable of these tasks were an option for the rest of us, but as soon as I realized it was feasible to do this kind of work in the comfort of your own home, I couldn't wait to start.

I would say that my work, like that of most designers, could be split into two distinct categories: commissioned work and personal work. Although I've worked in a diverse range of jobs and styles over the years – including graphic design, illustration (traditional and digital), interactive design, computer game development, and concept artwork – the distinction that has always stood out in my mind is whether the work is for others, or for myself.

In recent years, the bulk of my commissioned work has been in the form of freelance illustration. The work I'm generally asked to undertake is pretty well worked out in advance by the agencies' designers, and comes in the form of a very specific brief. From a creative point of view, this doesn't usually allow very much scope for experimentation; it's usually a case of carrying out the task expected of you. Personal work, on the other hand, is obviously entirely up to the individual, and therefore allows a lot more creative freedom and flexibility. I feel that the two are equally important in terms of broadening your experience, and both require their own set of disciplines.

When I was approached to work on this book, it felt quite different from anything I'd done in the past, because it kind of falls between the two categories mentioned above. Although I was working to a set theme, and there are obviously structures to be followed when you're producing a book, the design work itself was left entirely up to me. This made it quite tough to justify in my own mind what the work was trying to achieve.

When you're producing work for design/advertising agencies, it's quite clear that you're trying to advertise, promote, or sell something (a product, a service, or whatever). The work for this book, however, didn't share those goals. I was trying to communicate things like aesthetics, knowledge, and experimentation. (I was also trying to sell the book itself, of course.) This creative freedom is what made it feel more like a personal project than anything I'd been commissioned to do in the past – although I think it's interesting that I eventually found myself inventing a virtual company within the design. Was I trying somehow to justify the work as a 'real' corporate job?

Right from the outset, my thinking for this project was to produce a *series* of images, rather than working towards a single, definitive image. I was also very keen to design them specifically as pages *for* the book, rather than creating a series of images that would simply be featured *within* the book – and that meant finding out the page size in advance, and designing to fit those proportions. So although the ten designs that make up the 'work' represent the journey from initial concepts through to a final image, it was never my intention that the earlier images should be regarded as 'roughs' and the later ones as finished pieces. (In fact, some of the earlier designs are probably more valid, in that they're more closely related to the given theme. Later on, I decided to let the designs evolve, even if it meant straying from the theme a little.)

Five of the images in the piece I produced for this book feature robots, which I will discuss in more detail later on. Although I hadn't really thought about it until now, metal creatures seem to be a recurring theme in my work. I've produced quite a number of robots over the years, for both commissioned and personal pieces.

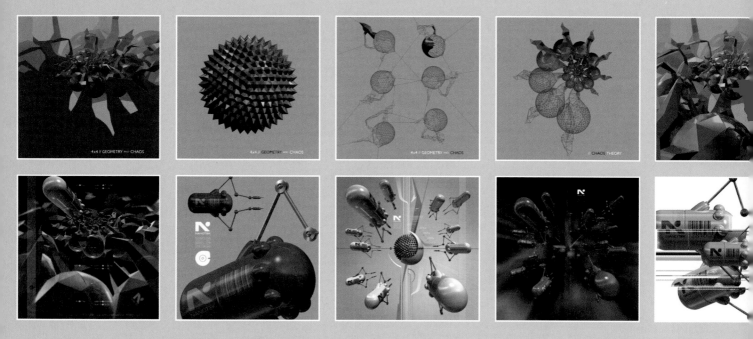

The *Retro Robot* image was one of six full-page illustrations that I produced for a large-format IT company brochure. The theme used throughout the brochure was science fiction, and the brief for this particular image was simply to feature a retro-style robot. I decided that it would be interesting to make it look like it was a cropped portion of a 50's B-movie poster, and I created the robot, flying saucers, and background mountains in 3D as separate elements that were then assembled in Photoshop. The text was imported from Illustrator, and various additional elements (including torn paper effects and creases) were added in Photoshop.

The *Robot Film* images are frames from a short movie sequence that I produced as a personal experiment for checking out a depth-of-field technique that I'll be describing in my tutorial. I felt at the time that photorealistic 3D work was often lacking in atmosphere, and this process gives it that extra spark of life. It's true that many 3D applications these days, especially at the high end of the market, do give you a built-in depth-of-field effect, but I still prefer the precise control you can achieve by doing it 'by hand'. This was the first time I'd tried out the process, and although this is a movie sequence, the principles are the same for still images.

A larger version of this image was later adapted for use as a splash screen for Pixelsurgeon (www.pixelsurgeon.com).

The *Rustboy* image shows the eponymous central character of my ongoing short-film project. I've been interested in animation and filmmaking since I was a child, when I got hold of a Super-8 film camera and fooled around with stop-frame animation using modeling clay. Later on, I progressed to foam-latex puppets with metal armatures. The problem was that the epic visions I had in my head were always slightly more adventurous than the equipment and budget would allow, so I never got much further than a few reels of animation tests. Those ideas lay dormant for many years, until the availability of sufficiently powerful computer technology persuaded me that it was time to have another try at producing a short film.

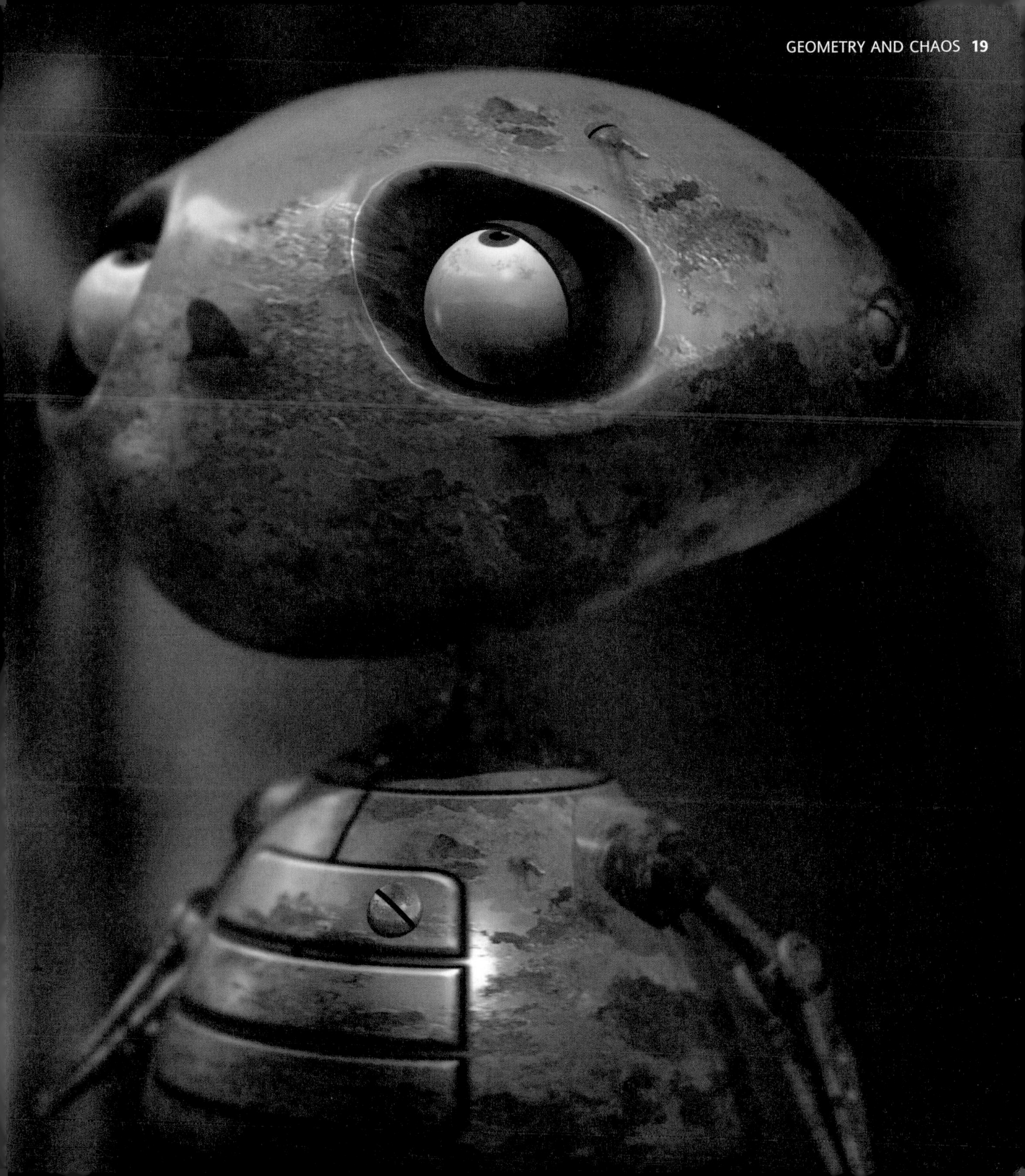

When I started work on *Rustboy*, I thought it would be an interesting idea to document the making of the film in some way, and after some consideration I decided that it would not only be my first attempt at making a 'real' movie, but also my first stab at creating a web site (www.rustboy.com). Putting my work online has been nothing short of a revelation, and it has opened up a lot of new doors for me. I'd long been a spectator of the online design community, but it wasn't until I got myself out there that I really appreciated the power of the Web.

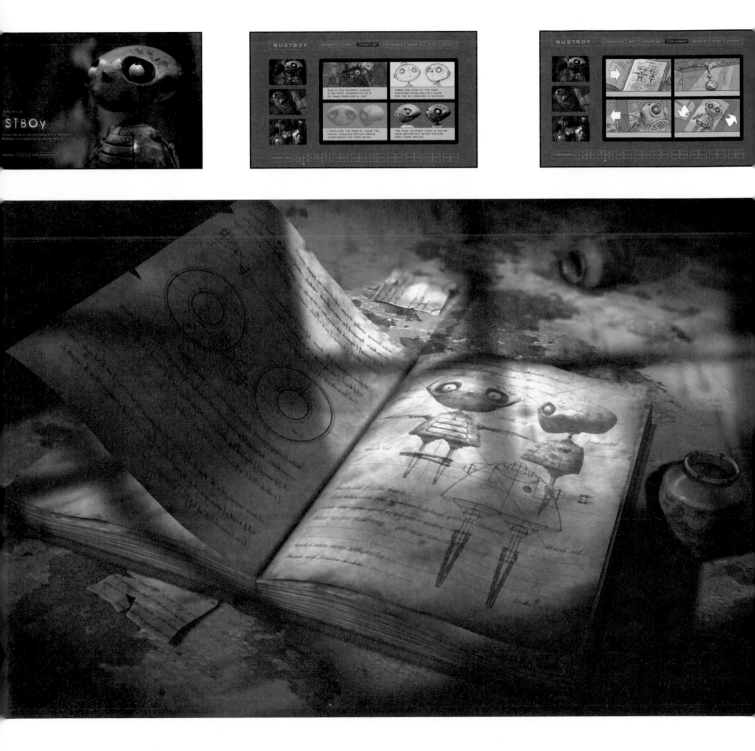

When you're doing the same thing day in and day out, I think it's very easy to get into a rut, and this is why I've tried to move between different fields of creativity. In that respect, 'going online' has been no different from any of the other sidesteps in my career, but it has certainly been the hardest hitting, and it feels like I've had a new lease of life. I have discovered the potential of the medium not only for showing your work to a (potentially) huge number of people, but also for helping, sharing, and collaborating with like-minded designers throughout the world. I've always felt that my best work has been done purely for the fun of it, and you only have to look around to see evidence that this is the case for other designers too. I quickly followed on from the *Rustboy* site by creating my XL5 web site, a space in which to exhibit my other personal work (www.XL5design.com).

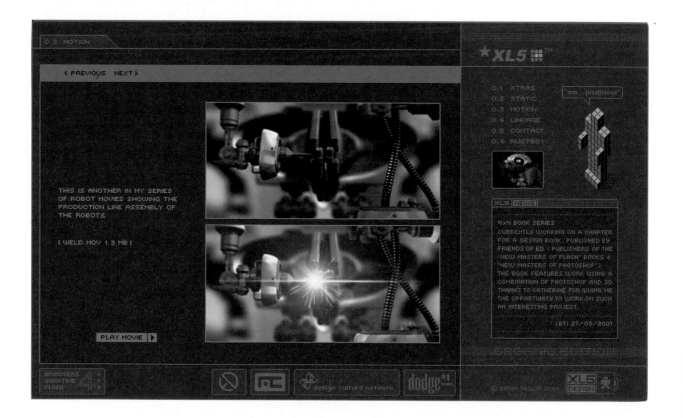

For example, one of the projects I set up through XL5 was *dodge* magazine, a quarterly, online design journal that was first launched in conjunction with design portal site kaliber 10000 (www.k10k.com). I started *dodge* for two reasons: firstly to allow myself a place to experiment with different styles and ideas from the work on *Rustboy*; and secondly to collaborate with other designers around the world, who were invited to contribute to the magazine. This is an ongoing project that I would like to see evolve, and I'm putting together the second issue at the time of writing this book. I'm very keen on the idea of collaboration, and the Web is the ideal place to make it work with relatively little effort. The book you're reading right now, for example, would not have been possible had it not been for the Web.

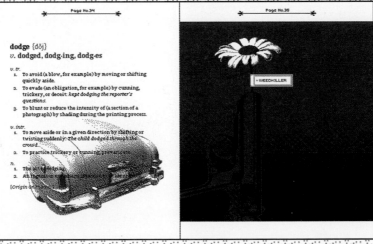

What about my work for this book? The theme was *Geometry and Chaos*, so the first thing I needed to consider was the relationship between these topics, and how I could approach them from a 3D perspective. Was it to be a comparison (geometry *versus* chaos)? Or some kind of combination of the two (geometry *within* chaos)? Or was it simply a case of illustrating both topics separately? In the end, my approach was not to be too literal about it, and I decided that the 'answer' was to be fairly unspecific about the relationship. As it turned out, though, I probably ended up addressing all of the above in one way or another.

The next thing I thought about was whether there were any differences between my understanding of the words in the theme, and their dictionary definitions. "Geometry" didn't turn up too many surprises; although there were a few variations, they all centered round the pure mathematics of points, lines, curves, and surfaces. "Chaos" can mean a state of extreme confusion and disorder, or else it too is used in mathematical terms (as in chaos theory). I was aware of both of these meanings and had already decided to incorporate them into my designs.

Even if a piece of work is eventually to be executed on the computer, I tend to start with some rough sketches on paper. I find that the sense of immediacy you get from a quick sketch can often give a piece of work more life, and tends to be less clinical than starting in the precise manner that working on a computer dictates. Because this piece was somewhat experimental, however, and the word "geometry" almost implies a 3D object, it seemed more appropriate in this case to dive straight into the 3D program and start the 'sketching' process there. I began playing around with some simple geometric shapes within Carrara's vertex modeler, and after a bit of experimentation I decided that my designs would be based around a sphere (or at least, around an approximation of a sphere made up of flat planes or polygons).

One of the objects that evolved from the sphere was a spiked ball shape, which to me visually encapsulated the word 'geometry', and which would be used in later designs to represent the geometric aspect of the theme. The precise composition and symmetry of this object could also be described as 'ordered', which I felt would be a good contrast to the chaotic part of the design.

If the spiked ball was to represent geometry, I thought it would be interesting to go back to the basic sphere and distort it in some other way to produce a shape that represented chaos. I did this by choosing random points on the sphere's surface and manipulating them in various ways to produce an asymmetrical object. I then expanded on the chaotic theme visually by trying to incorporate a suggestion of chaos theory into the design.

Chaos theory attempts to explain the fact that complex and unpredictable results can and will occur in systems that are sensitive to their initial conditions. I'm not going to go into a careful description here, but suffice to say that it's related to fractals – geometric patterns that are repeated at ever-smaller scales to produce irregular shapes and surfaces that cannot be represented by classical geometry. Gaston Julia, who gave his name to the Julia set, first discovered the principles of fractal mathematics as early as 1918. His work was essentially forgotten until Benoit Mandelbrot restored it to prominence in the 1970s, through his groundbreaking computer experiments. I wanted somehow to suggest fractal patterns in my designs, and this is what led to the spiral shape created with increasingly scaled-down and rotated versions of the initial 'chaos' object.

I liked the fact that my spiral scene, for example, looked very neat when viewed from 'above' – it had an almost natural form – but took on a much more random or chaotic look when viewed from different angles. Many people believe that the mathematical formulae that create fractal images are related in some way to the forms in nature, and are especially evident in things like ferns, snowflakes, trees, shells, etc.

It was around this time that I started playing with different color schemes for the spiral design. When I was working on the yellow version in particular, the objects looked to me like a mass of machines, which reminded me of the concept of nanotechnology – a subject I'd read about in the past and found very intriguing. If you haven't come across it, here's a dictionary definition:

Nanotechnology. A hypothetical fabrication technology in which objects are designed and built with the individual specification and placement of each separate atom. The first unequivocal nanofabrication experiments took place in 1990, for example with the deposition of individual xenon atoms on a nickel substrate to spell the logo of a certain very large computer company. Nanotechnology has been a hot topic in the hacker subculture ever since the term was coined by K. Eric Drexler in his book *Engines of Creation*, where he predicted that nanotechnology could give rise to replicating assemblers, permitting an exponential growth of productivity and personal wealth.

See also **Nanobot**.

Nanobot. A robot of microscopic proportions, presumably built by means of nanotechnology. As yet, only used informally (and speculatively!). Also called a **nanoagent**.

[Source: www.dictionary.com]

Phew, still with me? This was the thinking behind the later images in the series, and the reason for the 'Nanotek' logo, which was intended to represent a fictional corporation dealing in nanotechnology. This all seemed to fit quite nicely with the idea of chaos theory too, as both subjects are popular in hacker/cyberpunk subculture. I realized that this was getting away from the original theme, but I felt that since this was an experimental project, it was justifiable to let the concept evolve, and to veer off in whatever direction felt right.

I found this part of the process in particular very interesting, and would like to have taken it further still. I think that this is something you do automatically when designing – one thing very often suggests another – but only rarely do you do it as deliberately as this. The question is, if you do a series of designs in this way, letting one image influence the next, where do you stop? How do you decide when the work is finished? In the case of this project, that decision was made for me, and I knew I'd got to the end when I simply ran out of time. Ah, the finality of the deadline!

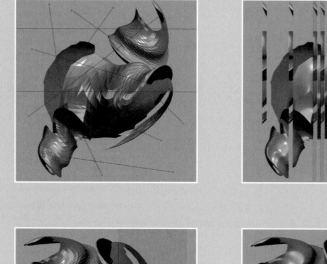

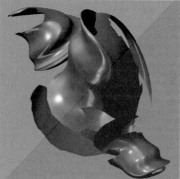

Looking at my designs in retrospect, I would say that I'm quite happy with the end result: things have worked out pretty much the way I intended. I would have preferred to take it a little further if I'd had the time, but the experience has nevertheless been an enjoyable one. At the time of writing this, I've no idea how the other three designers are going to tackle this project, or what kind of work they are producing for the book – but I can say that the direction I've taken has been partly inspired by the work of the others involved.

Although Dave, Nathan, and Tom all have their own distinct styles, I think that their work falls into the 'abstract' category. I like to work in all kinds of different 3D styles (realistic objects, Japanese-style cutesy characters, etc.), but I felt that in order to give the book a consistent feel, it would be a bit out of place if I were to go for something completely off-the-wall. As a result, I found myself working in a style that was similar in some ways to things I've seen in the others' work. Having said that, who knows what they're actually going to come up with – maybe they're thinking the opposite, and are planning something totally unexpected? Either way, I'm intrigued... and I'm very keen to see the results when all our work is put together.

4x4 // GEOMETRY AND CHAOS

4x4 // GEOMETRY AND CHAOS

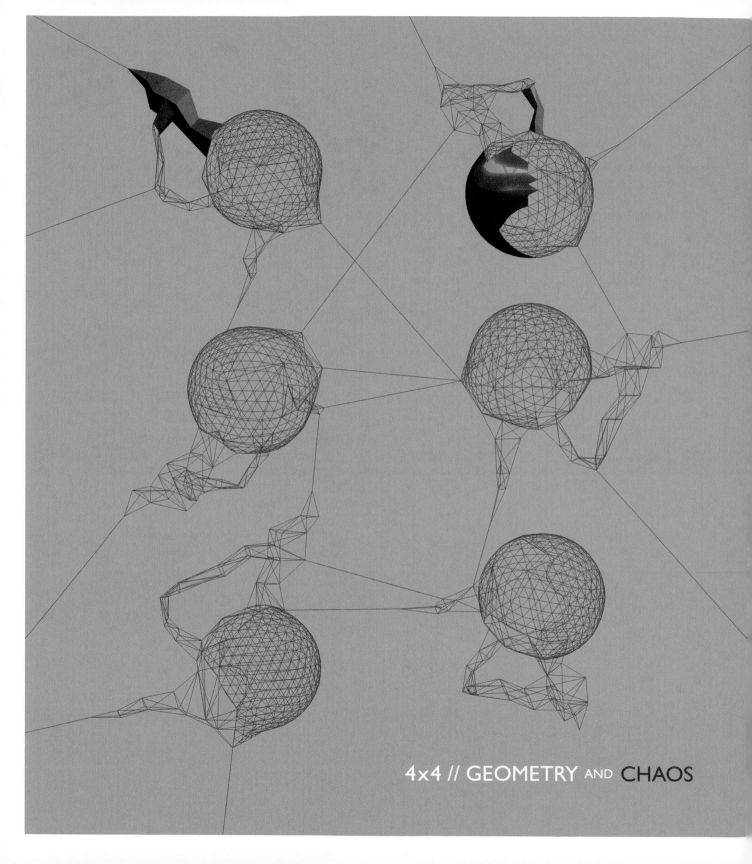

4x4 // GEOMETRY AND CHAOS

// CHAOS THEORY

2041-5179

NANOTEK

Mx ▬ 50nm   AssMblr Ct ▬ 40 000 000
                   ReplCtr Ct ▬ 80 000

MAGN ▬ 50nm   —   AssMblr Ct ▬ 40 000 000
                   ReplCtr Ct ▬ 80 000

Mx ▬ 50nm   AssMblr Ct ▬ 40 000 000
                   ReplCtr Ct ▬ 80 000

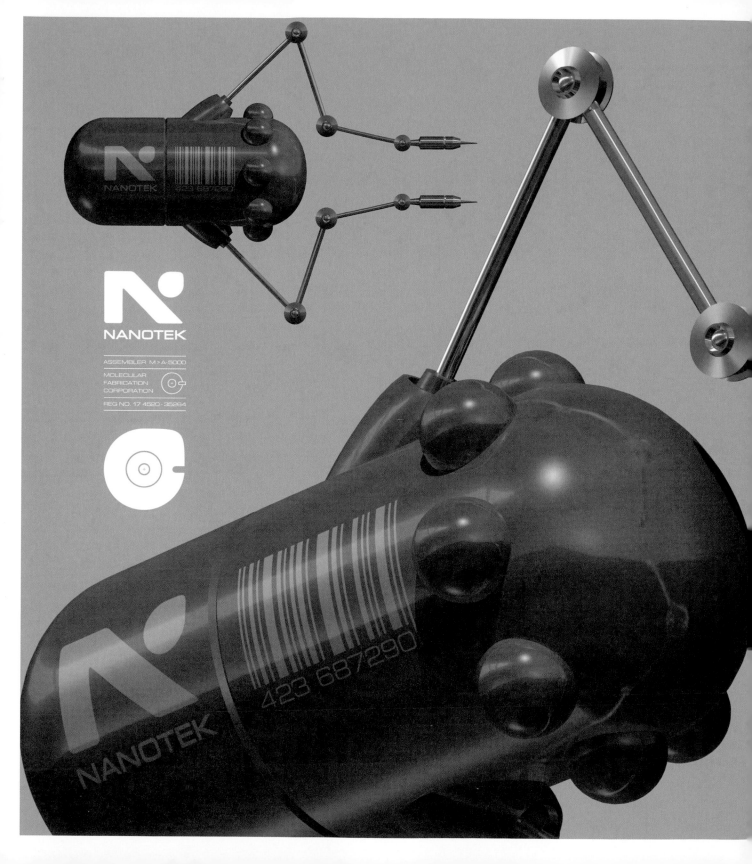

NANOTEK

ASSEMBLER M > A-5000

MOLECULAR
FABRICATION
CORPORATION

REG NO. 17 4520 - 35264

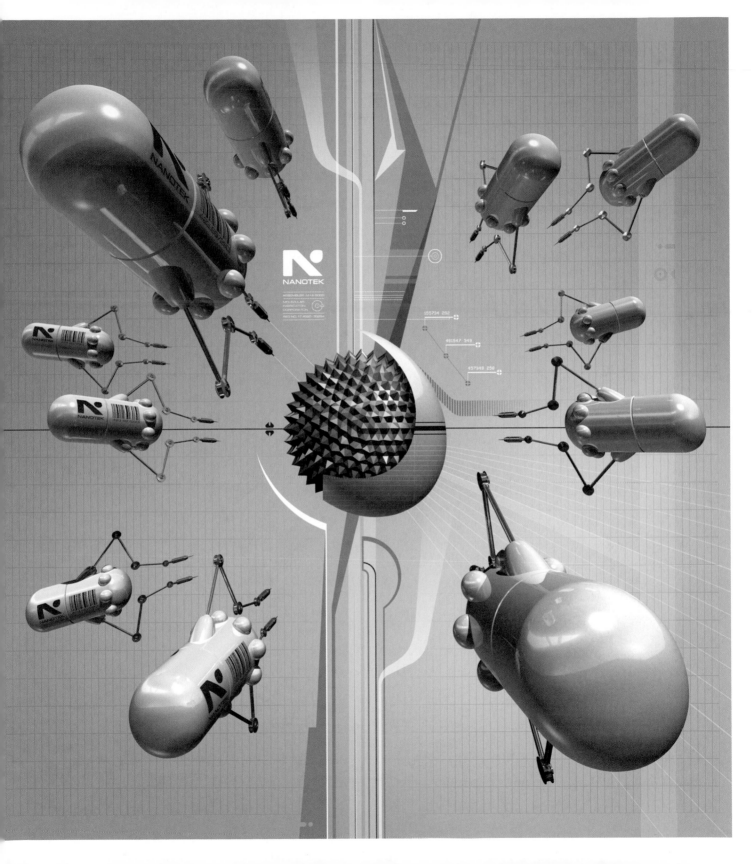

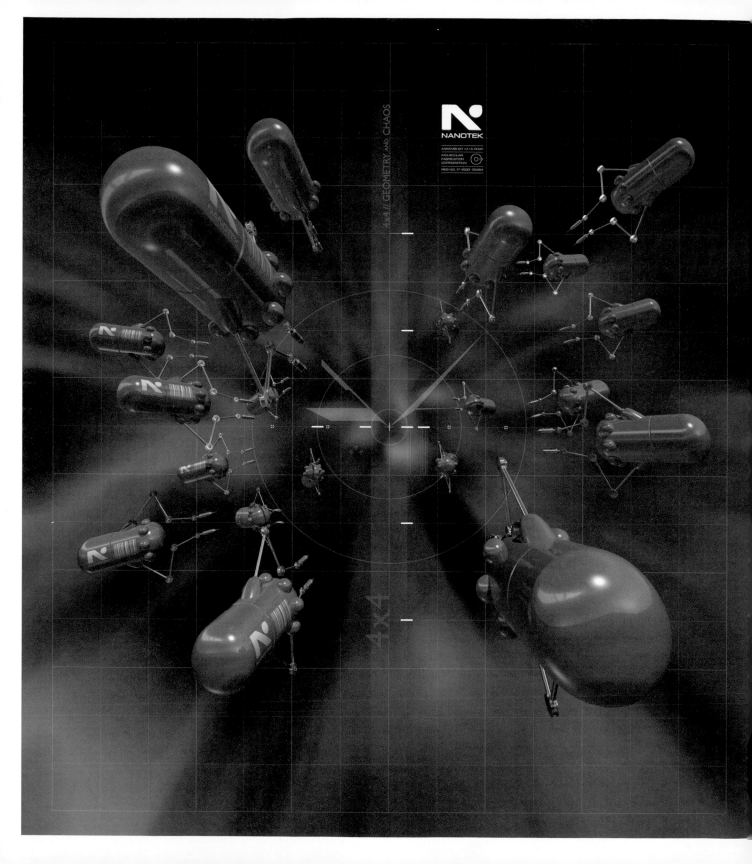

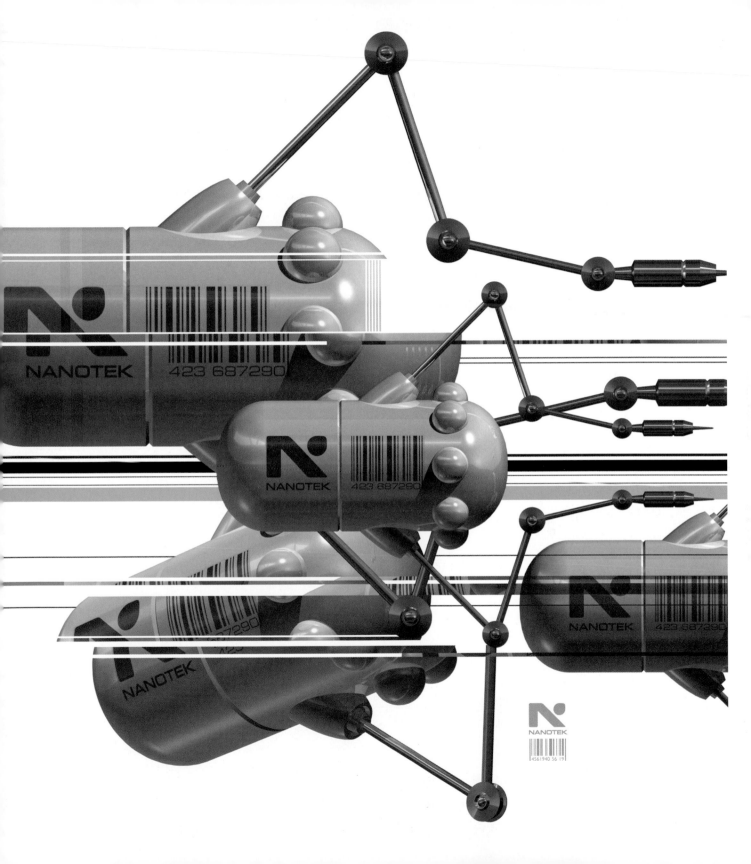

The use of Photoshop in conjunction with 3D software is something I'm very familiar with. Rarely do I accept something 'as is', straight out of a 3D software package – almost invariably, I'll post-process the image or movie in one way or another. In fact, Photoshop is normally used before and after the 3D process: before, for creating texture, bump, environment maps, etc., and after, for everything from simple color-correction to depth-of-field blurring techniques and additional effects or graphics. Photoshop plays a large part in giving my 3D work an individual look.

The 3D software packages I used for my piece in this book, and in the following examples, are Infini-D and Carrara. In truth, though, all the techniques illustrated here could just as easily be achieved in any 3D program.

Photoshop is one of those programs in which it's very easy to fall into the trap of just playing around to see what happens, and although you can get some interesting results from 'happy accidents' once in a while, I prefer to have a pretty good plan of attack worked out before getting started. This plan may take the form of rough sketches on paper, or simply having it worked out in my head, but it pays always to be thinking a few steps ahead – especially when you're using combinations of different software packages.

In general, the type of work I tend to do uses Photoshop in a fairly basic way. My style doesn't really call for lots of flashy filter effects, and an average job will involve using layer blending modes such as Multiply and Screen, and maybe a few simple blur filters here and there. Most of the work I do these days is for screen resolution rather than print, and as I'll describe later, I found myself using techniques that are usually associated with low-resolution work to get round some problems I encountered while creating the work in this book.

Because I elected to produce ten images for this piece, it would be impossible to explain every step of the production of every image in detail. Instead, I'll concentrate on three techniques that I use in my images in depth, and then talk through the creation of each of the ten images in a little less detail.

Depth-of-field effect

One technique that I like to use when trying to achieve a photorealistic 3D look is a simulated depth-of-field effect, where only certain elements of a scene are in full focus. The other objects are blurred by differing amounts, depending on their distance from the 'camera'. This simulates the effect you get in real-life photography, and it's particularly evident in close-up camera work – literally 'focusing' on an element is a great way of drawing a viewer's attention to a particular point in a composition. This is a method that I use extensively on my *Rustboy* project (www.rustboy.com), and I've also employed it in one of the images in this book (number six) to give the impression of a view from an electron microscope.

For this part of the tutorial, I've created a scene that demonstrates the effect more obviously. These are simply three shapes spaced equally apart, and the image below shows how they look when rendered normally. As you can see, each object is perfectly in focus at the moment, so what we're going to do is blur the foreground and background objects. The viewer's attention will be focused on the central object, for a more realistic, photographic look.

The depth-of-field effect is achieved by rendering the objects within a scene as different elements (or groups of elements) that can be taken into Photoshop as separate layers for individual treatment. (Note: many 3D programs have a built-in depth-of-field option, but this tends to have a significant impact on rendering time, and can yield unpredictable results. Using layers in Photoshop will give you much more control over the look of the scene and the intensity of the blurred layers, and rendering the individual elements will take a fraction of the time.)

The first step is to decide which object (or group of objects) should fall into which 'level' within your 3D scene, based on their distance from the camera. (I'm using three levels in this example, but any number could be used, depending on the subtlety of depth required.) This basically means drawing imaginary lines through your scene (three of them, in this case), and splitting the objects into associated groups. The three levels in this top-down view are the background (A), the middle ground (B), and the foreground (C). The camera is out of shot at the bottom of the scene, looking up.

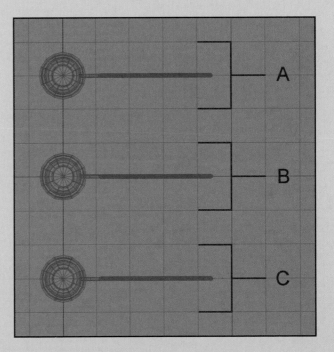

To render the background layer alone, I temporarily deleted objects B and C, and rendered object A using an alpha channel. Then I reverted to the saved version of the file and did the same to render object B, and repeated the process for object C. I now had all three objects saved as separate image files with alpha channels. (An alpha channel is a mask created at rendering time that represents the solid outline of your object with transparency information, in order that the object can easily be selected and copied when taken into Photoshop. The alpha channel will appear as a separate channel from red, green, and blue in Photoshop.)

Next, I opened all three of these files in Photoshop, and in each case went to Select > Load Selection. This uses the extra channel information to identify the object as a selected outline. Then, I copy-and-pasted the three images into three separate layers in a new Photoshop file (see image1.psd on the CD).

The middle layer was going to be used as the focus of attention, so that could be left alone. Rather, I selected the foreground layer, and applied a Gaussian blur (Filter > Blur > Gaussian Blur). I used a five-pixel radius in this example, but you can experiment with these settings depending on the intensity of the effect you require.

Now, selecting the layer containing the background object, I repeated the process. On this occasion, I used a seven-pixel radius for a slightly more pronounced blur, but again this depends on the effect you want to achieve; it would be just as easy to choose the foreground object as the focused layer, by applying a Gaussian blur to the middle ground, and a more intense blur to the background. This is what I meant about having more control than when using built-in depth-of-field effects. You can spend time experimenting with different intensities of blur, and choosing which group of objects to use as the focus of attention.

As you can see, this process has given the image a lot more depth. To finish things off in a more complex scene, you could apply subtle blurring to certain areas of the sharp layer in order to blend the layers together more convincingly. There are often cases where some objects (or parts of objects) in the sharp layer extend forward or backward to the 'borderline', so these areas can be selectively blurred to achieve a smooth transition between layers. The process looks obvious in the example shown here (for ease of explanation), but it can be really impressive when applied to a more complex 3D scene, and with a little experimentation can produce quite a photorealistic look to your imagery.

Creating accurate lines and grids

This section doesn't deal with a 3D-related issue, but it does cover something that I've found problematic when creating print work. Images six, eight, and nine feature lines and grids, which can be awkward to create when you're working on high-resolution pictures. The problem is that when you're working at high resolutions in Photoshop, you often have to zoom out to 16.7% or 12.5% in order to see the whole job on screen. When you do this, the limitations of a computer monitor mean that it can't accurately display fine lines, which will sometimes look thicker than intended, or even 'disappear' completely.

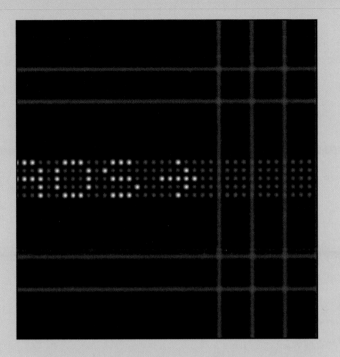

The way I got round this when producing image number six was by scaling the job down to 25% of the size I ultimately intended it to be, and saving this as a separate file. This gave me a picture to work with that was more akin to working on a screen resolution image, and allowed me to view the full job 'size for size', at 100% magnification. I was then able to work with the lines on a 'pixel graphics' scale, in a new layer that would later be scaled up and added to the original, full-size image. This procedure makes things much easier to work with, because you don't have the problem of lines 'disappearing' due to reduced magnification.

When the lines and graphics were complete and I was happy with all the line weights, I copied the layer and pasted it into a new file with a black background. (The graphics are white and gray against black, and later we'll use a Screen mode layer to 'burn' the lines through the original image file, so that the black ends up transparent.) The file was then flattened.

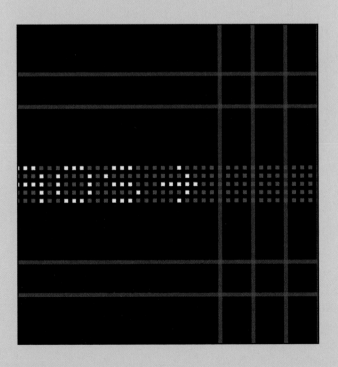

Because I'd originally scaled the image size by 25%, I needed to scale it up by 400% to restore it to its original dimensions. However, when the image is scaled up in RGB mode, Photoshop interpolates the lines, and they appear blurred.

The effect I wanted was crisp, sharp lines – so before scaling the image, I converted it to indexed color by going to Image > Mode > Indexed Color > Exact. This has the effect of limiting the file's palette to the exact number of colors used, so Photoshop will not (indeed, cannot) attempt to interpolate the lines when you scale up. Now the image will stay sharp when scaled, producing an accurate enlargement of the lines, without blurring.

Before leaving this example, I should point out that using this technique places a minimum weight restriction on the lines you create. In this example, because I eventually scaled up by 400%, no line in the final image could be narrower than four pixels. If you require *very* thin lines (say, one pixel wide), you'll have to create them at full size. Note, though, that such a line would be very narrow indeed when printed at high resolution.

Environment Map

All the 3D objects used in my work for this book have reflective, metallic properties. Creating a convincing shiny metal look can be tricky in 3D software, and it's particularly problematic here because my objects are rather abstract things floating in a void, when the appearance of a reflective object is actually defined in part by the environment around it. I'll use a real world example to explain this more clearly, before describing how to achieve the effect in 3D software.

If you imagine placing a chrome ball in the center of a real room, the ball would reflect everything around it – light sources, windows, objects within the room, etc. – giving it a shiny, metallic look. If on the other hand you had a completely empty room, with the walls, ceiling, and floor painted black, and placed the same chrome ball in the center, it would be very difficult to tell that the ball was chrome at all. It would just appear to be a black ball, having nothing to reflect on its surface.

This is the same situation we have in our 3D scenario: because the objects in this exercise have no environment around them, there is nothing to reflect. The way we get around this is by creating a 'virtual' environment. An **environment map** or **reflection map** is an image that represents the space surrounding our 3D object. Here's the environment map I created for use in all my 3D images in this book.

When you define an environment map for a 3D composition, it has the effect of wrapping the selected image around a virtual sphere, which then encompasses your scene. (Imagine a flat map wrapped around a sphere to represent the Earth's surface, but inverted so that the map is on the *inside* of the sphere.) This image will be reflected by the surfaces of your objects in the same way that a real room or landscape would.

Although the process of setting up an environment map will differ slightly from one 3D application to the next, you'll usually find it with the material/texture options – it's simply a case of importing an image to represent your environment. The pictures below show a rendered, reflective object without and then with my environment map applied.

Overview of the work

Having gone through those three underlying techniques, I'm now going to take you on a tour of the ten images that I created for this book, with a description of how each was made. If you'd like to experiment for yourself, you'll find the unflattened Photoshop files for all of these images on the accompanying CD.

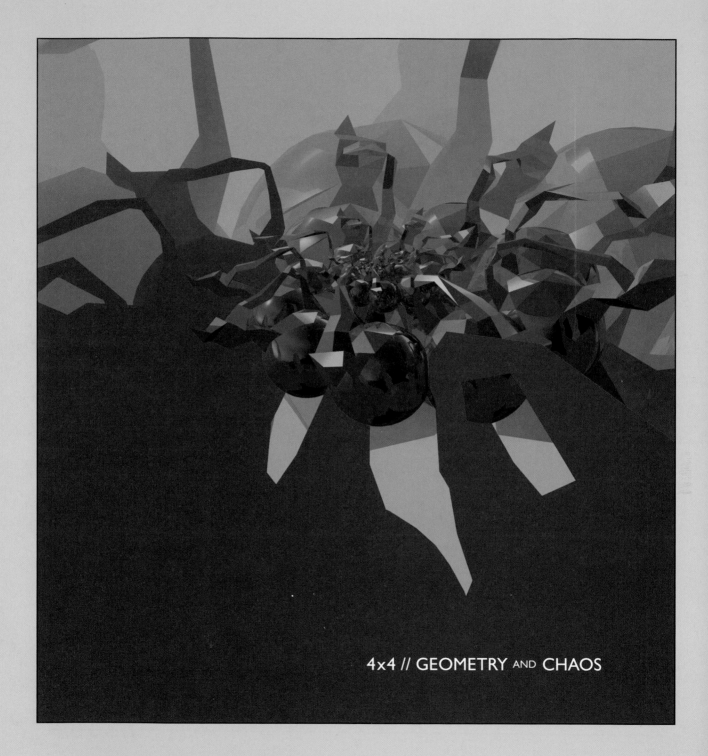

4x4 // GEOMETRY AND CHAOS

Image 1

This first image might look as though some Photoshop work was involved, but in fact the only element that owes its presence to Adobe's product is the text; the rest was created entirely within 3D applications. The object was modeled in Carrara's vertex modeler by starting with a default sphere shape, and extruding/pulling random points from the surface for a chaotic look. It was then saved as a DXF file that was later imported into Infini-D (the DXF file format provides a general means of transporting data between 3D applications).

After setting the material properties, as described in the 'environment map' section earlier, I duplicated the object. I then rotated and scaled the second object down slightly, and linked it to the original. The second object was selected, and the Duplicate as Child function was applied several times. This has the effect of repeating the changes made from one object to the next in incremental stages, so that each time you duplicate the object, it reduces in size and rotates by a specified number of degrees until all the objects eventually form a spiral. (See image number four for a top-down view of the spiral scene.) I then moved the camera around until I got an interesting view.

The red 'mask' effect was achieved in 3D by choosing several of the foreground objects, and applying a new surface map created within Infini-D. In the surface editor, I began by specifying the red color, and setting all the surface properties (diffuse shading, specular highlights, etc.) to zero. This has the effect of giving the object a completely flat look. Because all the surface properties were set to zero, light within the scene had no effect on the objects, and they appeared black. I then adjusted the glow properties until I achieved the desired shade of red.

4x4 // GEOMETRY AND CHAOS

Image 2

The model in this image was again created in Carrara's vertex modeler. I started out with a basic sphere, with the default number of polygons (60).

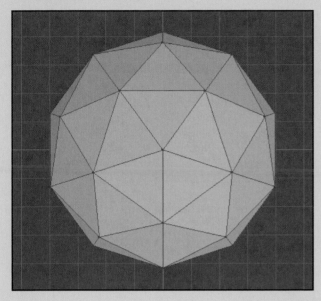

Next, I subdivided the object twice, to create more polygons.

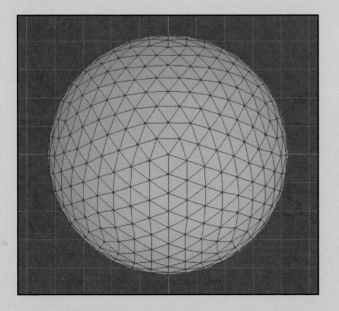

At this point, I selected the entire sphere, and saved the selection (Selection > Save selection). I then subdivided the sphere once more, creating an even greater number of polygons.

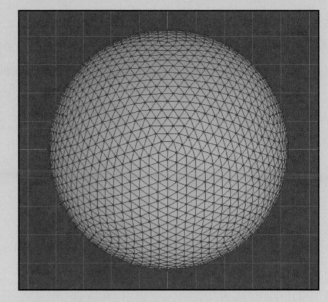

I then selected the previously saved points by going to Selection > Restore selection.

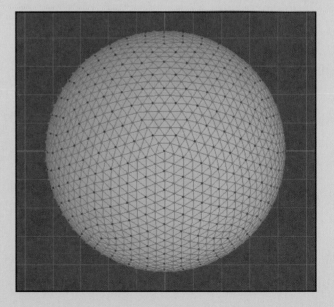

With these points selected, I scaled them by 110%, with Selection > Resize. This had the effect of pulling the selected points out to produce a spiked ball.

The model was then saved as a DXF file and imported into Infini-D, where the chrome texture was applied. This was one of the base objects that I would use in later images.

Image 3
This image shows the individual object that was used in the spiral scene from various different viewpoints. I rendered two versions of this scene: one in wireframe mode, and the other fully shaded. I took both versions into Photoshop as individual layers, and selected portions of the shapes on the uppermost, shaded layer by using the Polygonal Lasso tool that's obtained by holding down the Option/Alt key. I then inverted the selection and deleted the unwanted portions, revealing the wireframe version underneath. The connecting lines were simply drawn on a new layer with the Line tool.

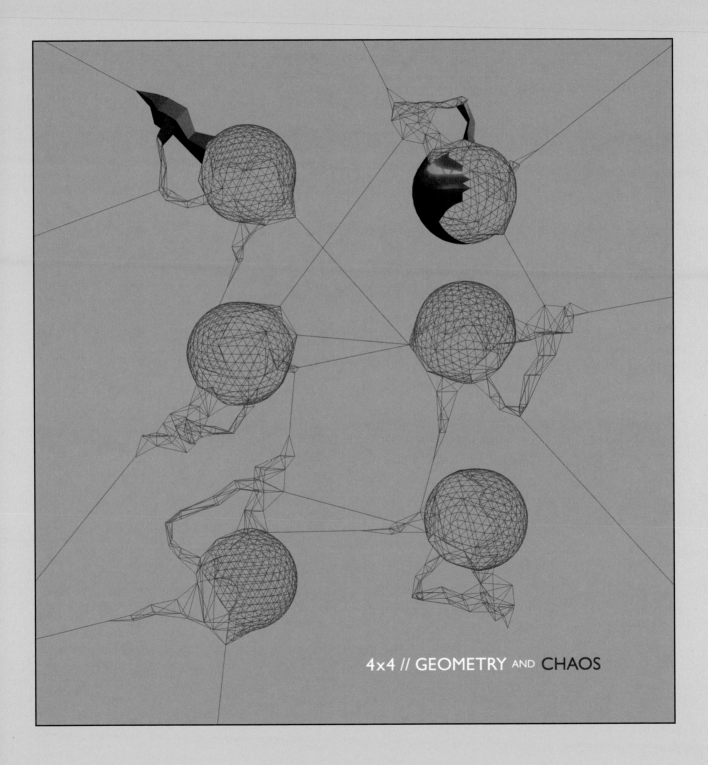

4x4 // GEOMETRY AND CHAOS

Image 4

This is the top view of the spiral scene, as described earlier. It was created in a similar way to the previous image, by placing the wireframe and shaded versions on different layers in Photoshop. This time, I drew a diagonal selection through the center of the spiral on the uppermost layer, and used a large feather value on the selection to achieve a gradual blend when the unwanted portion was deleted.

// CHAOS THEORY

Image 5

This design uses the same 3D scene and viewpoint as the first image, but at this stage I started to experiment with different color schemes in the 3D application's surface editor. Here, I used 'fog', with the color set to the same value as the background in order to diffuse the distant objects, blending them softly into the background for added depth. I added the logo and line graphics in Photoshop by placing an Illustrator file and using the Distort tool to match the perspective of the surface to which it was applied.

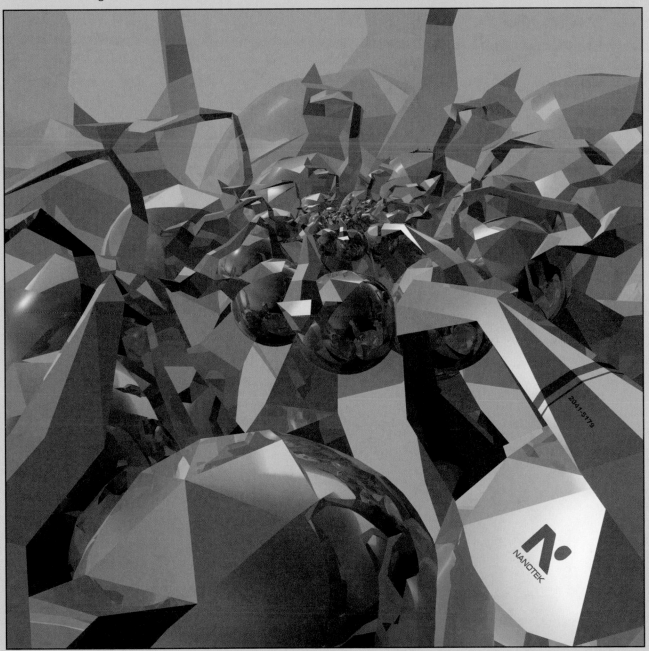

Image 6

I started to experiment a little more in Photoshop at this point, by blurring layers for a depth-of-field effect, using the technique I described earlier. The overlaid graphics were created directly within Photoshop on separate layers, using Screen mode to 'burn' the images through the underlying layers. The white robot was a later addition; I decided to include it in this image after creating it for the next one in the sequence.

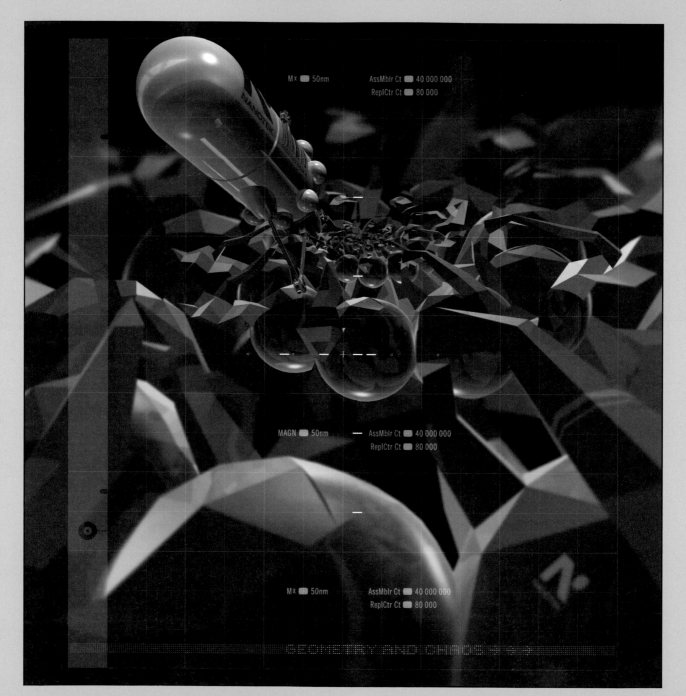

Image 7

This page features my nanobot model, which was created very simply by using lathed objects for the pill-shaped body and arm parts, with spheres around the shoulders.

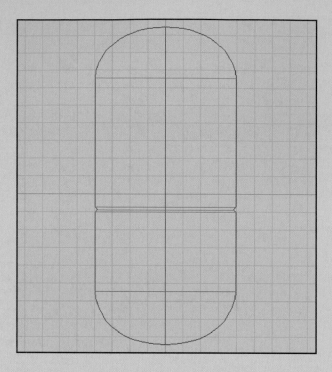

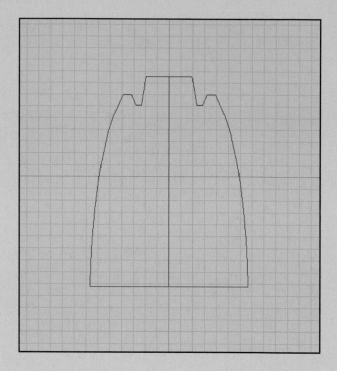

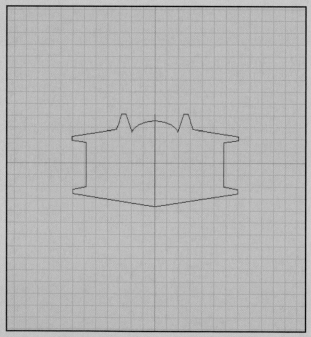

(A lathed object is achieved by sweeping a path around in a circle to produce objects such as pots or bottles, similar to the way you would create an object on a potter's wheel.)

The "Nanotek" logo and barcode were produced in Photoshop and used as texture maps that were applied to the model within the 3D application. I rendered two versions of the model from different viewpoints using alpha channels; these were then pasted into layers in Photoshop so that they could be positioned separately for the desired composition. The final step was to place the white graphics into the image, which were created in Illustrator.

Image 8

This is one of the more elaborate designs featuring the nanobot models. In this image, they were all rendered together in one scene within Infini-D, so that subtle reflections were caused from one to another. I created different-colored variations of the logo and the barcode texture for this model because I wanted the finished design to have a cold, clinical feel to it.

As usual, the scene was rendered with an alpha channel for ease of composition when opened in Photoshop. The only thing required for this layer was some subtle color correction, and to reposition the bots slightly in order to create a more interesting composition. All the additional graphics, lines, and grids were drawn directly within

Photoshop on various layers, using either Multiply or Screen blending modes, as described in detail earlier. The spiked globe was used as the focus of attention in this design, while the 'shield' shape was 'stolen' from part of the bottom-right nanobot image. (An example of something that *was* just one of those happy accidents.)

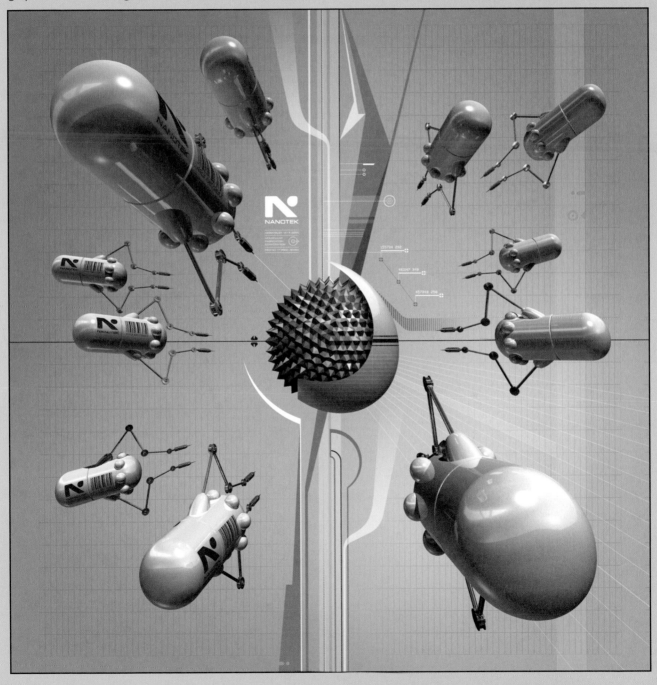

Image 9

A very blurred version of image number six was used as the background for this design. First, I applied a radial blur (Filter > Blur > Radial Blur > Zoom) set to the maximum value of 100, followed by a Gaussian blur with a seven-pixel radius, to soften the image. The overlaid lines and graphics were achieved using the same methods as described in the previous image.

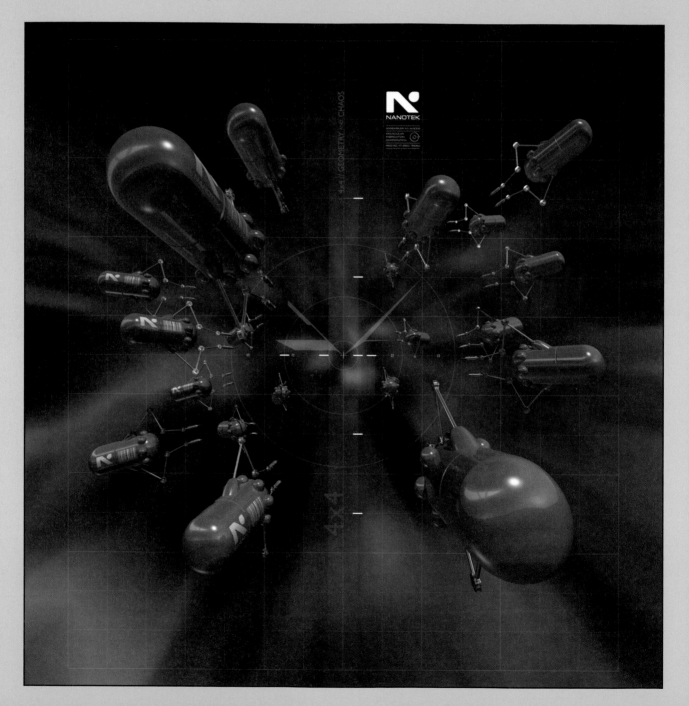

Image 10

The final image used models from a side viewpoint that were rendered with an alpha channel and placed on different layers in Photoshop. I then used the Rectangular Marquee tool to chop the layers into slices and offset them in various ways. The red portions of the design were produced by first desaturating the image (Image > Adjust > Desaturate), then filling with the red foreground color, making sure the fill mode was set to Screen.

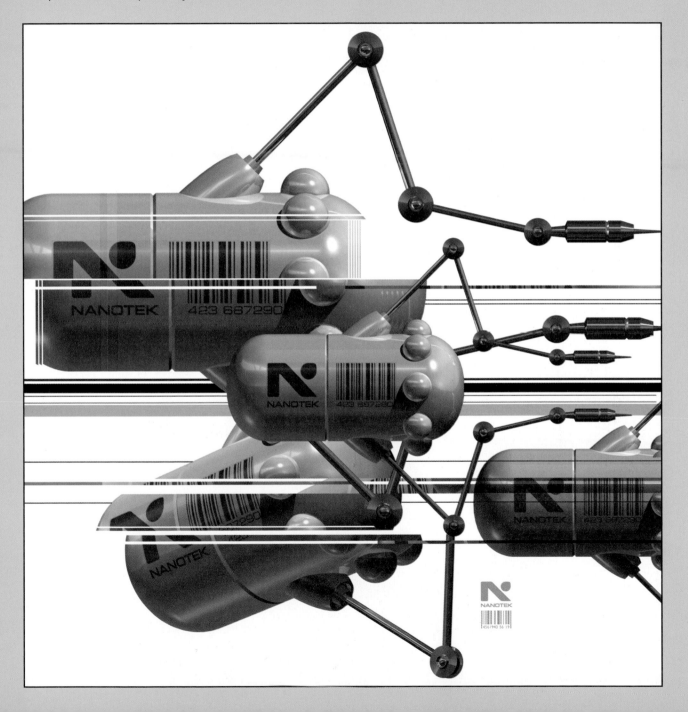

Final words

I think that the most important thing about working in Photoshop, 3D software, or any other creative computer application, is to find your own style of working. Hopefully, you'll find some of the tips I've presented here useful, but they're not intended to be a step-by-step guide to creating exactly what I made. Rather, they're a starting point for your own ideas. If you want to develop an individual look to your work, my advice is not to take the accepted capabilities of a piece of software as read, and restrict yourself to those boundaries. Decide what you want to achieve first, and figure out a way of making it happen. If it's easy to get the latest cool effect by simply clicking a button, remember that there are thousands of other people who are capable of clicking that button too.

BUT WHERE ARE YOU GOING?

take the reader on a journey

There's a certain amount of irony in the fact that at the very moment I was invited to collaborate on this project, I was busily deleting a couple of folders' worth of useless 3D objects from my library. It's an occupational hazard: I tend to stockpile loads of stuff that will never see the business end of a PSD file, and from time to time I'm forced to obliterate it, or else I'd be left with very little drive space. This systematic eradication was also partially motivated by the fact that I was bored with the direction I had taken with respect to 3D design, and I wanted to try out a few different methods. *Geometry and Chaos* provided me with that outlet at a very convenient time.

At times, this project seemed to be nothing but a collection of lengthy pauses and brief flurries of production – but then, that's exactly how everything I make ends up getting done. I just sit around until something hits me in the face, and then I fall into a concentrated spell of action. At the end, I often can't remember how I got there.

There's a scrap of paper on my desk that says, "Take the reader on a journey," and another scrap not too far away that reads, "But where are you going?" For me, the most important stage of this particular journey was the documentation of the creative process. It was relatively easy, in theory at least, to sit back and let my hands adjust a few pixels here and there; the real challenge was the words, and how to approach the narrative.

This brick wall led me to push aside my keyboard and start making lists, and these in turn led to short, fragmented paragraphs. I regarded these scraps of text and grammar as I would regard index cards, like the ones people use for public speaking. The outline was there for reference, but they required a voice to flesh them out and give them some purpose. Even though I knew that translating my code-like notes and collections of fractured memories into something recognizable was going to be a serious pain in the rear end, it really should have been easier than it was. All I had to do was to go through what I did and what I was thinking step-by-step, and write "the end" when I had nothing left to say. The only problem is that if you were to break it down into bullet points, this essay would look something like this:

1. Received the theme from the friends of ED. I think I'm going to like this project.
2. Started to work. Stopped. Played some Mario golf and drank a few beers.
3. Started to work. Stopped. Played some Mario golf and drank a few beers.
4. Worked out some ideas on about 50 pieces of scrap paper and 30 square feet of whiteboard. Looks good. I deserve a beer.
5. This 3D stuff just isn't working for me.
6. Played some Mario golf and drank a few beers. I got my first ace!
7. Found a slightly more useful useless 3D object to work with in my 3D library.
8. Tweaked the file and exported some images from 3ds max to use for the design.
9. I like Photoshop.
10. I'm done! What are the other guys up to?
11. What the hell am I going to write about?
12. Played some Mario golf and drank a few beers.
13. Writing is hell.
14. The end.

I wouldn't call that interesting reading! One of my half-baked theories was that somehow, the title of this book had found its way into the joints of my fingers and the folds of what I now loosely refer to as my brain. At times, the given theme seemed all too appropriate, and on a number of occasions I was even ready to substitute the word "geometry" with "frustration"; "chaos" was the only theme that seemed to require no invitation to the party. Some brainiac out there would be sure to point out that unknowns are the soul of chaos, but I *hate* those gray matter types.

One thing I *do* know is that for me, the creative process is never a linear journey, and I always find a way to get distracted and end up some place completely unexpected. Admittedly, I tend to like that feeling of surprise, so maybe I'm instinctively putting myself in situations that will create those moments of creative disorder. I just wish that I could consistently recreate the sequence of events that leads up to me staring at a finished Photoshop canvas with a smile on my face.

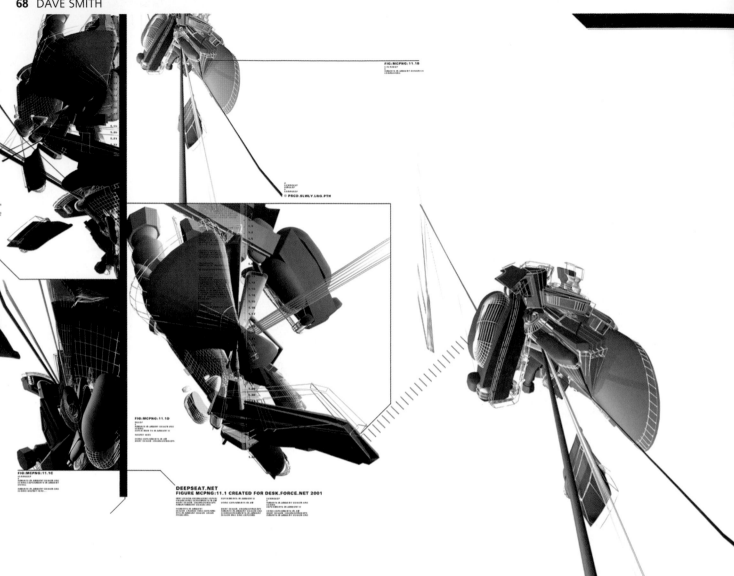

FIG:MCPNG:11.1B

PRCO.SLWLV.LNG.PTH

FIG:MCPNG:11.1D

FIG:MCPNG:11.1C

DEEPSEAT.NET
FIGURE MCPNG:11.1 CREATED FOR DESK.FORCE.NET 2001

To accompany this essay, I've provided a series of images, both previously seen and unreleased. I first started using 3D elements in my design work in 1999, when I was studying new media – using 3D Studio Max formed a part of the curriculum. Initially, I hated the program, but after a lot of experimentation I grew to like the abstract shapes and effects that I could generate and then subject to further manipulation in Photoshop, which was a program that I had already become familiar with. It was from this point that I began generating massive quantities of what I referred to in the first paragraph as "useless" objects, for use in conjunction with my design work. When you're looking at the pieces I created when I was a student, though, please be kind – I was inexperienced!

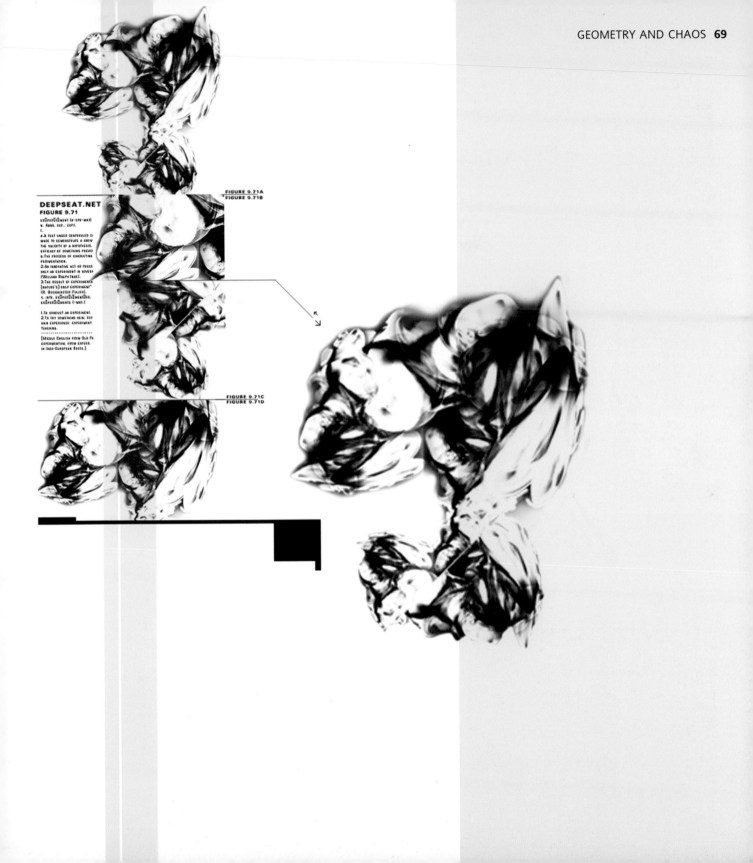

DEEPSEAT.NET
FIGURE 9.71

ex·per·i·ment [ɪk-ˈsper-mənt]
n. Abbr. exp., expt.
1.
a. A test under controlled co
made to demonstrate a know
the validity of a hypothesis,
efficacy of something previo
b. The process of conducting
experimentation.
2. An innovative act or proce
only an experiment in govern
(William Ralph Inge).
3. The result of experimenta
(nature's) only experiment"
(R. Buckminster Fuller).
v. intr. ex·per·i·ment·ed, ex·
ex·per·i·ments (-mənts.)

1. To conduct an experiment.
2. To try something new, esp
one experience: experiment
teaching.

[Middle English from Old Fr
experimental, from experir,
in Indo-European Roots.]

FIGURE 9.71A
FIGURE 9.71B

FIGURE 9.71C
FIGURE 9.71D

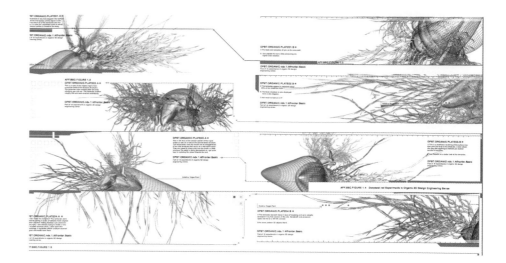

I freely admit that apart from being pretty nifty to look at, the stuff I was creating in Max back then didn't serve any real purpose. What I was learning during that period was how to use Max, if not in its fullest sense, then at least in a way that would allow me to develop increasingly complex models through simple processes. As I was doing this, my comprehension of Photoshop and other graphics and animation programs such as Fireworks, Flash, and Illustrator was also continuing to mature.

Plate 01

Plate 02

PLate 03

Plate 04

Plate 05

Plate 06

Plate 07

Plate 08

Plate 09

Plate 10

My one problem was that I felt I had got myself stuck in a rut. I wasn't happy with the work that I was developing because it seemed to be a repetition of similar forms, and lacked an overall notion of true complexity. I consciously started to try and develop some guiding concepts, and working through a series of narrative styles and visual explorations, I hit upon the notion of treating 3D shapes as objects to be examined in a series of textbook-style plates. The idea would allow me to develop relatively basic models, and then to experiment with more abstract ways of displaying the imagery, with the objects at the center. Replicating the style of a science book, and messing about with the typography, layout, and the 3D subject matter became something that I was excited about. www.deepseat.net became the venue for my 3D work, and for various other experiments with 3D design.

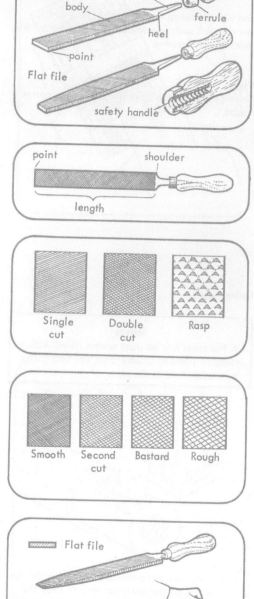

Files

Files are manufactured from hardened steel. Teeth are cut on the body in various patterns and the file is used by hand for the removal of metal.

Identifying Files

To identify any particular file it is necessary to know:

the length,
the type of cut,
the grade of cut,
the shape.

Length

The length of a file is measured from the point to the shoulder.

Type of Cut

The most commonly used cuts are single, double and rasp.

Grade of Cut

Files are cut with teeth of different grades. Those in general use are smooth, second cut, bastard and rough.

The Shape

Flat File

A flat file is used for general surfacing work. Both faces are double cut, and both edges are single cut. It is tapered in width and thickness.

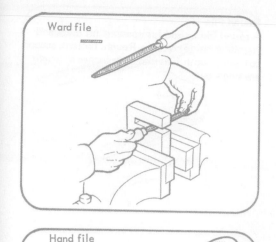

Ward file

Ward File
A ward file is used for filing in narrow slots.
Both faces are double cut, and both edges single
cut. It is tapered in width but not in thickness.

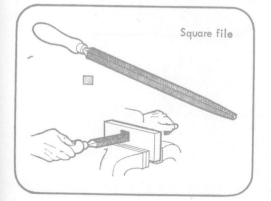

Hand file

Hand File
A hand file is used for general surfacing work.
Both faces are double cut. Either both edges are
single cut, or one is uncut to provide a safe edge.

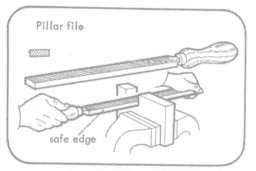

Pillar file

safe edge

Pillar File
A pillar file is used in narrow slots. Both faces
are double cut, and either both edges are single
cut, or one is uncut to provide a safe edge.

The way that my science textbooks presented information
has always stuck with me, and to this day I can spend hours
in bookstores poring over them – the fact that I failed at just
about every science and math course you can take during 20
years of education is something I look back on with some
amusement.

Square file

Square File
A square file is used in corners. It is double cut
on all sides, and is tapered.

The pure theory that these books contain appeals to me, and
while I may not be up on my table of elements, I do at least
have a layman's comprehension of chaos theory – and that
made the concept development part of this assignment a
little easier. Somewhere early in the concept phase, I fell for
the idea of position as an element of pattern recognition. The
idea of systems interacting with one another to form a
greater system was an aspect of the theme that I wanted to
exploit in the 3D portion of the construction.

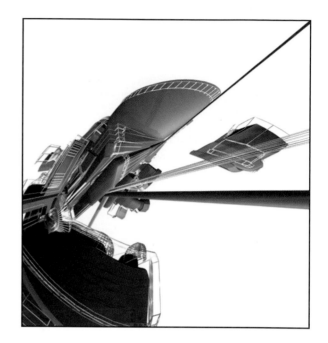

If you want a good example of this, take a look at these two different renders. They have the same structure, but the different camera angles reveal two completely different-looking figures. Furthermore, the point of view became an essential part of this approach to chaos theory. 3ds max would become the avenue by which I would explore the concept of pattern recognition, and Photoshop was to become the way that I would pin down the more chaotic themes by injecting very strict geometric shapes into the mix.

The theme of *Geometry and Chaos* was open to a wide range of interpretation. However, having already worked out an underlying concept that would inform the project, I thought that I could simply fire up 3ds max and start working. Right away, I began generating irregular shapes and filling the file with cameras that I hoped would converge to form an original structure. As time passed, I thought that things were starting to come together, but the test renders revealed that some more thought was required. I decided to shut everything down and began to do some more brainstorming about the topic and possible structures.

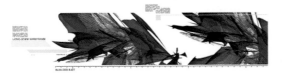

Whiteboard#2 with G&C Project Notes

I'd already outlined what I was going to do in my head, but I needed to write it down somewhere in order to keep me on target. There's no better surface for this than a whiteboard: you can pour your brain out onto a larger-than-life format, and selectively erase any offending parts with ease. In this larger format, it all came to life for me.

3D Station: Dell P3 -700//17" Dell Monitor

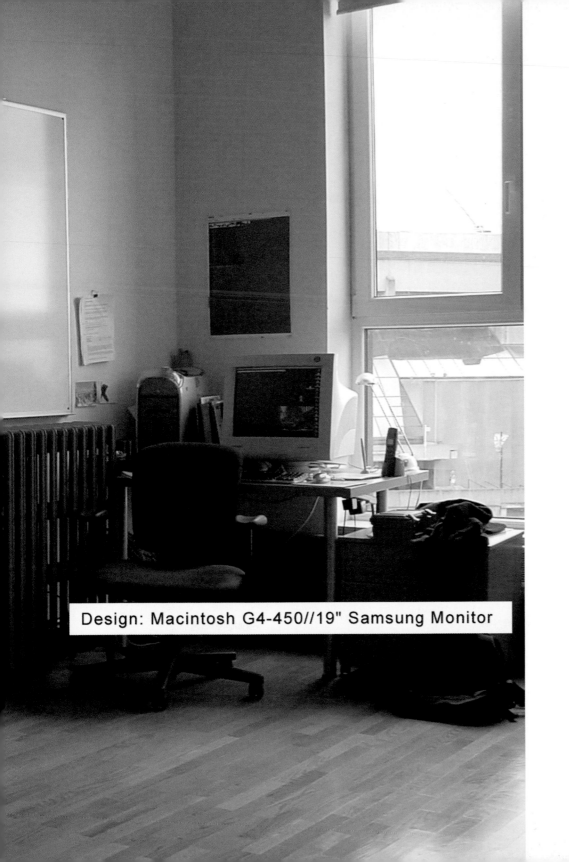

Design: Macintosh G4-450//19" Samsung Monitor

My original theories that individual structures or systems would affect each other, and that camera position would dramatically influence an individual's point of view, seemed to be workable and – more importantly – thematically correct. It was also during this phase that I stared exploring different and more rigid geometric shapes than the ones I had used in the past. I felt that organic structures were contrary to the theme, and that objects based on architecture would work better. It was also a direction I hadn't considered before, and I was excited about pursuing it.

The bases for this excitement were the architectural works of Arthur Erickson, who has designed some of the most visually stunning buildings in my home city, Vancouver BC. His work is pretty hard to miss – it stands out against the vertical glass-and-steel architecture that's so popular here. The easiest way to see some of it is to visit his web site at www.arthurerickson.com, and from the images there it's plain to see why the structures would have been attractive to me. The buildings themselves are beautiful, but his work is really a study in how people react to certain environments. They provided me with inspiration regarding possible forms, and showed me how seemingly separate geometric structures could interact to create a complete system.

This concept of interacting structures was part of my underlying idea for *Geometry and Chaos*, although I was more concerned with the idea of perspective *creating* form, than with functionality *dictating* it. I also thought that having these structures all around me would provide enough inspiration to make the construction phase easier, and it was starting to look as though all this preparation would pay off. Wrong. This was actually where the frustration factor really started to kick in. I felt like everything I was making was derivative, and I definitely felt like I needed a break from all things computer-driven.

I came back to work on the project a couple of days later, refreshed after doing nothing creative in the intervening period. (At the time, my day job didn't count, because I was simply attending corporate meetings and working on concept development. After three days of paperwork and project briefings, I was ready to do something completely out of step with the boardroom.) But when I sat down to work, I just wasn't able to get the 3D stuff working. After two more days, and with my deadline looming, I decided to toss aside my chosen subject matter and instead looked for something usable in my library of miscellaneous organic renders and 3ds max files.

Eventually, I retrieved an old file that had been scheduled for termination. After finding it in my junk folder, I gave serious thought to never tossing anything out ever again. (Idiot! What else have I deleted?) The object was pretty straightforward, the result of some experiments I was doing a while back with 3D flower structures and different methods of applying materials. After I went through the file and removed all the extra lighting and environmental effects, I realized that it contained many of the key ideas that I had wanted to explore for this project in the first place! (The proper word to inject here would be "lucky".) After this conceptual and structural barrier had been removed, I began to work with the file and exported a number of different PNG sequences that I was then going to trim down to a single graphic to be used in the Photoshop portion of this assignment.

The underlying concepts for this piece worked their way to the surface completely by accident. I was crossing something out, when I noticed the effect that the big boxes of fill I was using were having on the sketched 3D shape. I felt that there was a tremendous opportunity to fuse the key thematic ideas so that they played off each other more harmoniously. Once again, I pulled ideas from plates in old science textbooks, where organisms such as butterflies and beetles were often tacked down with pins and bits of tape. These creatures were immobilized for photographic purposes, and I felt that the blocks of fill were accomplishing the same effect: it didn't feel like the 3D elements were separating from the page, as they sometimes had in the past. Using the organic piece also allowed me to use more irregular lines, and to separate the strict geometric forms that I wanted to place on top of the 3D elements.

Experimenting with a variety of different possible executions, I quickly put together three or four different layouts using my predetermined thematic concepts. Each had varying degrees of complexity, and all of them reflected my ideas of pattern recognition and geometric fencing – but only one of them had the percentages right. In other words, only one of them was subtle enough with respect to the desired geometric organization, while at the same time not relying too heavily on the 3D elements to hold the viewer's attention. The images that follow show a few of the semi-completed pieces that I worked with, as well as the completed piece.

4

x

There's too much chaos here for my liking, and the only things to be carried over into the final design from this first image were the colors that I used. I felt that the 3D elements were far too disorganized, and the blocking wasn't accomplishing what I wanted it to.

Geometry and Chaos

4

4X4 VISUAL EXPLORATIONS

Again, I really liked the color combinations in this image, and I was tempted to run with it to completion, but something about it felt wrong, and I wanted to explore some different ideas with regard to layering and the 3D elements. Eventually, I all but forgot about this piece, which is why it appears so unfinished.

4

x

Geometry + Chaos

The colors in this image are pretty awful, but I really like the way that the definition of the 3D object has been totally obliterated, leaving only the vague impression of the structure's outline. This was a key element in the final design, and the blocking – although extreme – was beginning to pin down the 3D elements in the way I had planned.

4

Continued experimentation led me to this final design. I liked the basic aesthetic, and I felt that the chaotic 3D elements were working in unison with the geometric shapes that were meant to add some measure of control. I know I'm done when I can sit there and restrain myself from making changes (or if I'm making changes just for the sake of moving a pixel here and a pixel there, as was the case with this design). This final image is this piece that I called *Geometry and Chaos*.

4

X

4

In the past, I had held up 3D objects like the one in this image as things worthy to be examined in their own right. In this piece, I wanted it to be a part of the whole, rather than the focus. I was counting on this approach to make my work a little different from the things I'd done in the past, but I didn't want it to be a total departure either. I was also hoping not to overshadow the required theme of the project. Finishing this part was quite a relief, and there's a fairly enthusiastic check mark on one of my lists, noting its completion!

But what were the other three guys up to? Based on their previous work, I had some assumptions as to the nature of their designs, but I wasn't sure how they would interpret the theme of *Geometry and Chaos*. Brian is an awesome modeler, and has uncanny abilities with regard to textures and depth of field. Having seen www.xl5design.com and www.rustboy.com, I'm expecting his piece to be quite complex, and to feature a range of different subject matter. Tom is an amazing designer in the classical sense. He gives fantastic treatment to type, and I've long been impressed with his ambient 3D work. Based on *his* earlier stuff, I'm expecting to see something mathematical, which leads me to believe that our approaches might be the most similar of the four contributors. Nathan has a complete disregard for the conventional uses of typography, color, and environmental effects so I'm assuming that his piece will be visually rich. I've been a fan of his abstract work for a long time, so I know his stuff is going to be strong.

One of the most exciting things for me is the fact that I've been given the opportunity to work with people for whom I have a pretty high regard, and it's this fact that makes the possibilities presented by the collaborative portion of this project so exciting. The way I look at it, cracking this book open might generate the same mixture of excitement, fear, humility, and embarrassment that ran through me when I first received my invitation to contribute to this project.

Looking back, I know that I'll recall how the theme dictated more than just the direction of the artwork. My life was corrupted by it for a few short, enjoyable, but frustrating weeks. I still kind of wish that the written aspect of this piece had flowed a little more smoothly, because I know that there are huge gaps in the bulleted list that I've tried to flesh out. For me, chaos crept its way into the geometric shapes of these keystrokes and letters, and I can only hope that my narrative hasn't been lost in a garble of fragmented thoughts and misplaced adjectives. But then again, sometimes it's fun being cryptic, especially at the end of a journey. Writing *is* hell. The end.

4X4 VISUAL EXPLORATIONS

4

x

Geometry + Chaos

4

x

Geometry and Chaos

4

X

4

Individual:Deepseat:Net%Project:FourXFour%Theme:Geometry%and%Chao

My first reaction to having to write a tutorial was a mixture of fear, confusion, and humor – but mostly confusion. I consider that to be a perfectly natural response, though, because even having been forced to document my methodology for this project, I still quite honestly have no idea how I do things. I *think* that I approach the creative process with the same method as anyone else: if I don't have a preconceived concept, I usually just sit down and start making stuff, and hope that something will squirt out the other end. During my usual construction phase, the 3D and layout issues usually just work themselves out, and ultimately I just hold onto the hope that I'm making something coherent and visually pleasing.

The shapes I create are usually just abstract twists and bends, brought together to resemble something coherent. I don't consider myself to be great a 3D artist by any stretch of the imagination, but I do have a passion for the medium, and for those same randomly twisted shapes. As a result, this is not a traditional tutorial. I've consciously written it as a travelog of my motivations and practices, rather as than an instrument of pure instruction. My theory is that the journey will provide its own instruction, and that you'll take away something meaningful despite the relative lack of technical description. The notes I took over the course of this ordeal are fairly complete (if cryptic), but I've divided the sequence of events into three parts. These sections are directly related to the programs and stages of production as I traveled from station-to-station and platform-to-platform.

Concept development
(or, Forming the required intent)

themes... failures... lists... ideas... whiteboards... concepts... sketchbooks... subject matter... flowerbeds... systems and chaos... it might be useful someday

Staying true to my usual line of attack, I began working in Max, hoping that something vaguely related to the theme would take form. After several failed attempts, however, I decided that some more thought was required. A series of lists, and illegible notes scattered on scraps of paper, whiteboards, and sketchbooks followed closely behind this impulse.

My first step was to break the theme down into two columns with the headings *Geometry* and *Chaos*, and then to start writing down anything I felt was relevant to each topic. I find that by taking the time to do some basic analog brainstorming, I get all the monkeys shaken out of the tree, and I can see better what I'll have to work with.

Under both headings, the words and phrases that I ended up thinking were most relevant were "form", "shapes", "position", "without form", "pattern recognition", and "systems". I then went about placing the words into different sequences, and brainstorming about possible thematic ideas. A basic concept developed, revolving around the idea that objects randomly placed within a confined area would interact to form new, original structures or recognizable patterns (something like looking at the sky and seeing clouds that look like a duck chasing a monkey). Broken down into their base elements, those clouds are just collections of frozen water molecules forming random patterns against the sky. Furthermore, a viewer's position will affect what they see in that particular cloud formation.

Continuing to work out a way to approach this subject, I moved on to a larger, messier step in my evolutionary process: using a couple of whiteboards located in my studio. I started by sketching out some concepts of placement, with little or no thought going into what the shapes I was going to create would resemble. Going back to my lists of key words and phrases, I decided to see if this idea of position and pattern recognition was something I wanted to go after. As it turned out, I liked the possibilities the concept presented, but I still didn't know what the individual structures or systems were going to be based on.

As I said in my essay, it was at this point that I became inspired by the work of Arthur Erickson. I visited his web site, and toured some of his buildings, and even went so far as to create some composite sketches like this one, influenced by what I had seen.

But then I scrapped this idea, because it sucked. I do that a lot, and consequently I spend a lot of my time building mockups for sites that will never be carved up and coded. It drives me crazy, and wastes disk space – but why should this project be any different from what I usually work on?

In the end, I decided to go with an idea that I had worked on before and was comfortable with. On that occasion, inspiration had come from a group of flowers that I'd once seen in a flowerbed. I'd found that standing in different positions in relation to the bed allowed me to see different patterns in the flowers. Considering this, and looking back on my notes, my final definition of the theme became, "Depending on a particular point of view, objects placed in relative position to one another will interact to create a new, original structure." To me, this encapsulated the system-to-system interaction that I understood to be at the heart of chaos theory. As it turned out, I even had a file that fit these parameters perfectly in my library of Max work. If only I'd realized that sooner...

Creating geometric chaos: 3ds max

violence solves at least one problem... orientation... station-jumping... mario golf... quad patches... free form deformation... camera position... exporting sequences... cameras, lights, and the FFD 4x4x4 modifier... transferring

If anyone ever tells you that using elements created in 3D application in your work is a cop-out, punch them in the head. The legal department at friends of ED may not like that incitement, but there it is. 3ds max and the other industry-standard 3D programs like it are massive, and I'm pretty sure that the only people who *really* know the ins and outs of these monsters are the people that created them.

My monster of choice is Discreet's 3ds max. It has a fairly usable interface, and it's the simplest of the 'serious' 3D programs that I've used. (I've experimented with Maya, Strata, and Softimage as well, but I didn't take to them – Max was the first I was exposed to, so I have a soft spot for it.) In addition, peripheral programs and plug-ins (such as Vecta3D-MAX and Swift 3D MAX) make it that bit more flexible. What I like about these 'extras' is that they allow you to model something in Max, and then export animated sequences or stills that can be imported into Flash or Director as vector animations, or into Photoshop as design elements. That kind of feature can add further depth and life to a web project, which is essentially why I began using Max in the first place.

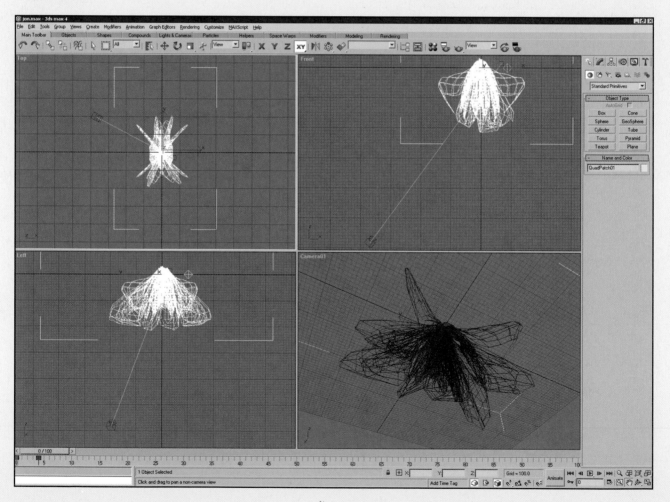

A demonstration version of 3ds max can be ordered from Discreet's web site at www.discreet.com.

As a 3D artist, I only use Max at the most rudimentary of levels. My thinking is that if I keep things as simple as possible, I have a greater chance of success. In case you've not seen it before, I'll begin here with a very quick tour of Max's interface, in order to familiarize you with some of the terms and palettes I'll be using later on.

The tabs that run across the top of the 3ds max window provide quick access to the tools and objects that are used most frequently when you're modeling. These are complemented by the set of smaller tabs that runs down the right of the screen; the settings available here allow further specification of the choices made from the 'quick' tabs – or else, if you wish, you can start from the more detailed set straight away.

The most obvious features in the user interface, of course, are the four view ports in which all modeling and animation occurs. Your default views are 'Top', 'Front', 'Left', and the fourth window (bottom-right) that starts with a 'Perspective' view, but has been changed in the screenshot to display the view from a user-positioned camera.

Immediately below the view ports is the animation timeline, which is activated by turning on the large Animate button toward the bottom-right of the window. Moving the scrub bar along the timeline and then selecting a view port will allow you to move objects within the scene; any camera or object movement will then create a keyframe at that point in the timeline.

This has been a quick-and-dirty look at Max's most salient features, but I'll be going into greater detail as the tutorial progresses. In creating this part of the tutorial, I found it necessary to outline what things I did, and how I did them, as two separate parts. Subsequently, I've tried to interlace the technical and personal narratives into one coherent journey. My hope is that beginning with 'why things happen' will lead more easily into the 'how' of this particular project.

After the trials and tribulations described in my essay, the file that ended up becoming the central element for my contribution to this publication was one that I created about a year and a half ago, called `some_flower2`. Through some magical twist of fate, it had a lot of the key elements that I had outlined in my initial notes; I found that the pieces did indeed change dramatically in appearance, depending on which of the multiple camera views I was using. This kind of system-to-system (or object-to-object) interaction was exactly what I'd been hoping for from the outset.

Collectively, the file is pretty much just a bunch of quad patches (see later) that I rippled, tapered, and then further subjected to freeform deformation. That may sound kind of heavy, but I've constructed a rough sequence of how such a structure might be created that I'll take you through. The process is really fairly simple, and it starts, as you'd expect, with a new Max file.

Modeling

For test purposes, and for models such as these, I like rendering against a white background. I usually intend for the models I create to be looked at from several different angles, so a true 3D environment with texture maps and so on is generally not required. Using white also comes in handy later in the design phase, as I tend to work against light colored backgrounds once I get into Photoshop, too. Choose Rendering > Environment, click on the Color swatch in the Background field, and reduce the Whiteness to pure white.

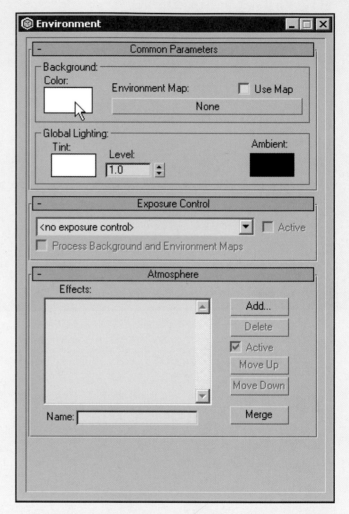

Once you've done that, select a Quad Patch object from the Modeling tab at the top of the screen, and introduce it into the scene via the Perspective view port. By entering values in the Parameters section of the Modify tab on the right of the screen, you can make the patch any size you like; I made mine 200 x 200.

Also in the Parameters section, bump up the length and width segments to around 10 per side. This will give your meshes more flexibility, and greater possibility for detail. (This is essentially the same thing as bumping up the number of sides on a sphere that's made up of polygons, to give it a smoother appearance.)

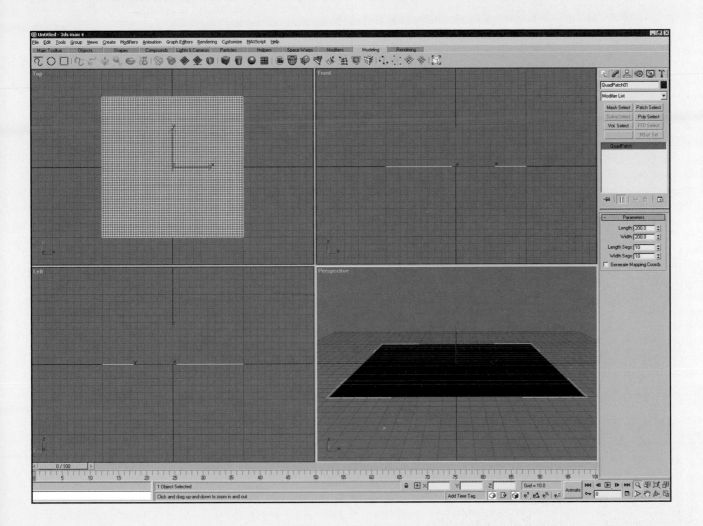

Making sure that the object is still selected, select the
Ripple modifier from the Modifier List. In the Parameters
section, adjust the values of Amplitude 1 and 2 until there
is a dramatic wave structure in the quad patch. It can be
as large as you want, but I don't like to go too crazy – I
used amplitudes of 20 and 30 respectively.

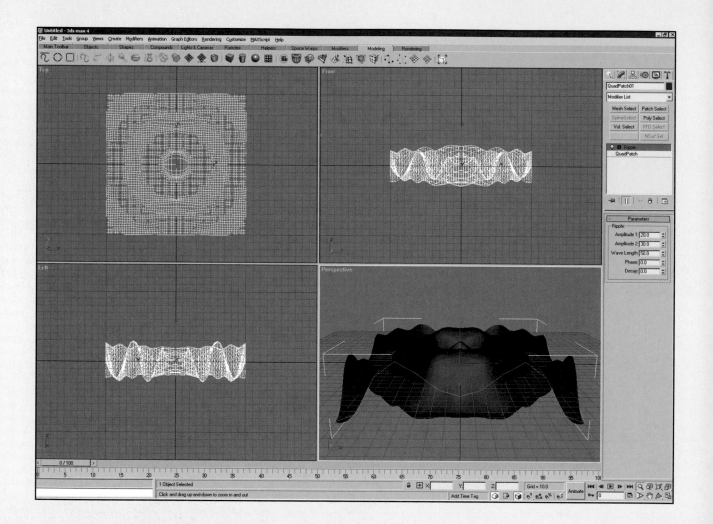

Next, select the Taper modifier and collapse the object in on itself until you get a bowl-like shape. I used an Amount of –2, and then flipped the Perspective view on its head by using the Arc Rotate tool from the bottom right of the screen.

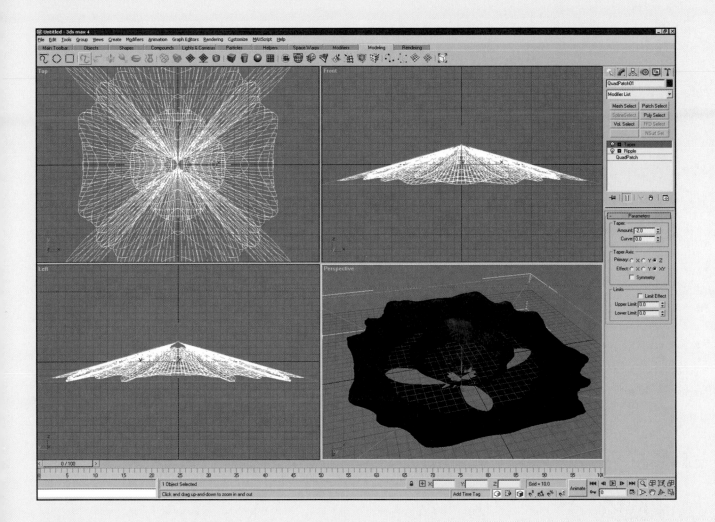

Then, choose the Free Form Deformation 4x4x4 modifier; you'll see an orange box structure made up of intersecting boxes and lines around the quad patch. Select the 'select and move' tool, and right-click in the Perspective view; you'll see a menu that looks like this.

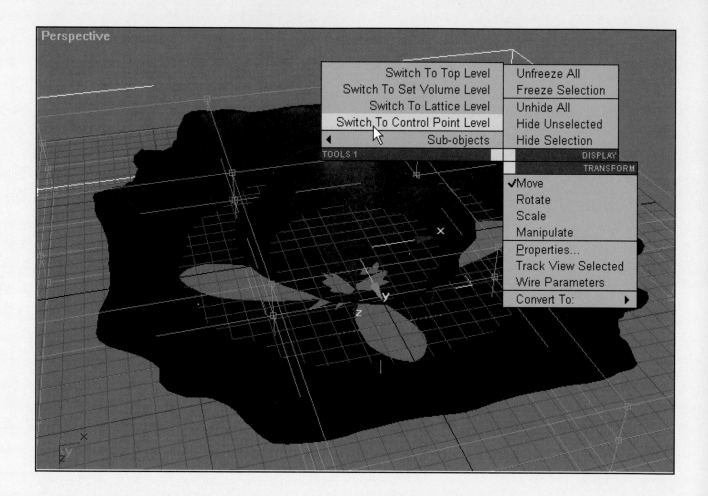

Once you've chosen the highlighted option, you can start pulling and twisting on the control points on the various axes in various view ports, until you get a shape that you like. Hopefully, a petal-like structure will begin to emerge – but it's all a matter of time and experimentation, so don't be surprised if it doesn't look like anything much for a while.

Materials

The 'materials' that I've used in this project are actually just different coloring effects, applied using the Material Editor's most basic functions. Applying materials to an object can be as basic or complicated as you want; I tend simply to use matte colors. By playing with different color combinations in the Ambient and Diffuse fields, you can often get some original effects.

Select the Material Editor from the Main Toolbar (it's the four colored balls). Then, choose any of the colored balls at the top of the dialog box, click the box marked Ambient, and select a color from the palette. Then repeat this step for Diffuse. (I usually select a color analogous or opposite to the color in the Ambient field, but that's just me.)

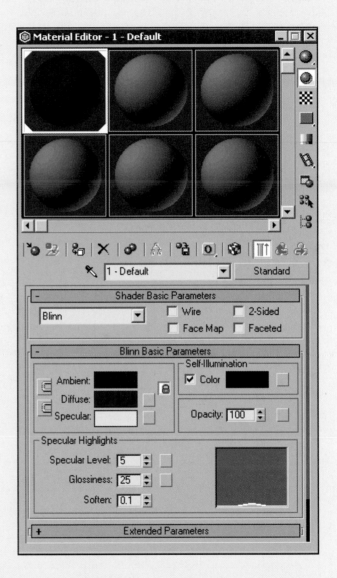

Next, select Wire and 2-Sided in the Basic Parameters section of the editor, and assign your new material to the 3D object by clicking the appropriate button (the little circle with the little arrow pointing at the square).

The Material Editor itself is huge, and any number of pre-defined materials can be selected from the libraries. To view the standard library, click on the ball with the arrow pointing at it; selecting any of the items in the dialog that appears will display a preview of the material on a ball.

The colors I've used for this example are pretty standard, but I knew that the addition of lighting would dramatically change the appearance of the object anyway. In addition to this approach, I'll sometimes play with the opacity, luminosity, and specular levels of a material, in order to create different shading effects. By playing with any of these, you're affecting the way that the material will react to light. In the case of some_flower2, I had simply used color combinations in the same ways that I've loosely described previously.

Lighting

Lighting the scene was accomplished simply by dropping 'omni' lights above, below, and on all four sides of the object, at distances roughly equidistant from its center. Unlike spotlights, which focus a beam of light on one particular area, omni lights are just simple light bulbs that illuminate a general space. You can spend an entire 3D career learning how to light a scene properly, but I'm not doing anything dramatic here. My main goal was to simply illuminate the object from all sides, so that I could get an even distribution of light over its surface.

It's important to note that once you introduce your own light to a scene, you lose the default lighting that you've used for modeling. At this point, I recommend saving your model as a separate file, and using a copy to add your lighting. In fact, I'd do the same before introducing a new camera, or doing any animation.

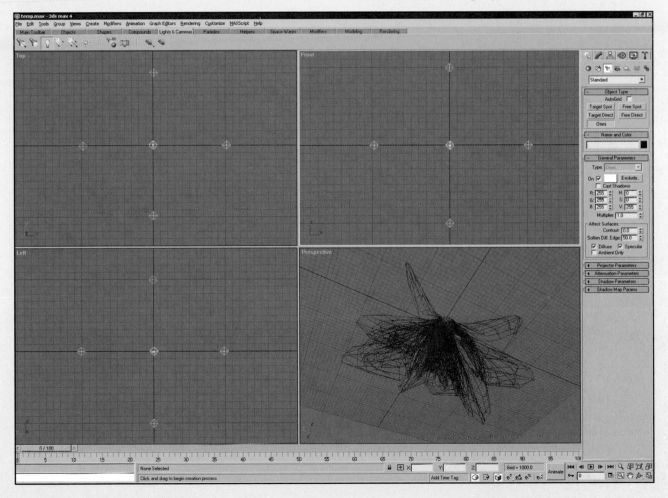

In the Top view port, zoom out some little distance, and select the Omni Light from the Lights & Cameras tab at the top of the screen. Then, place lights at 90-degree angles from each other, surrounding the object. In the Left view port, place two more omni lights above and below the object, making a total of six in all. If you need to, reposition the lights so that they're roughly the same distance from one another.

You'll notice that the object has become over saturated with light. To fix this, you can either move the lights farther away, or you can modify the amount of light that each source is spitting out.

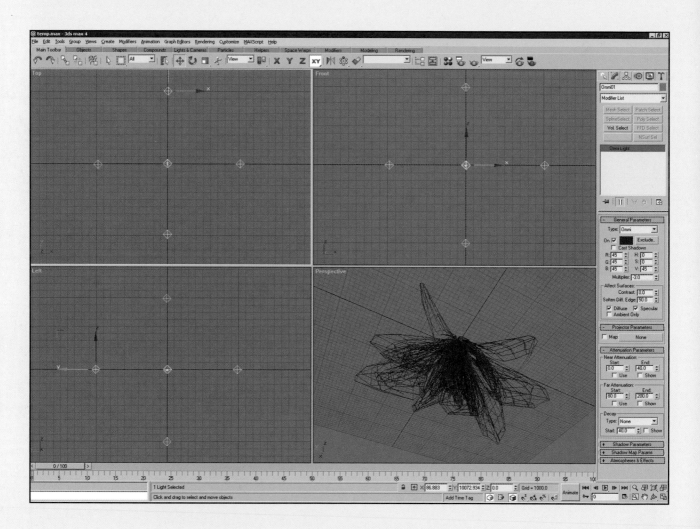

To achieve the second of these, select any omni light, and take a look at the General Parameters section of the Modify tab. As well as changing the color of the light, you can use the Multiplier setting to affect the *amount* of light being emitted. From this basic starting point, it's quite good fun to move the lights around, and to experiment with different shadows, and how they play off the materials that you've used.

Cameras

My next step was to load the file with a bunch of cameras of arbitrarily selected focal lengths and types. To do this, select Target Camera from the Lights & Cameras tab, drop one into any of the view ports and draw out the field of view until the camera is 'seeing' the object.

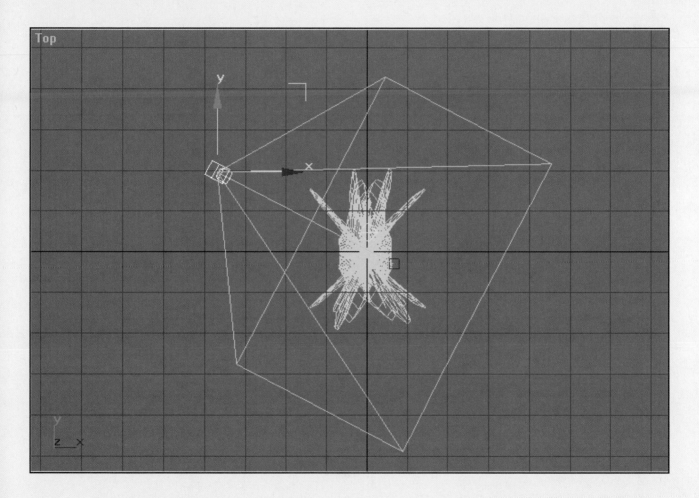

Then, to see the camera's view in your Perspective view port, right-click on the view port's header, choose Views from the pop-up menu that appears, and select your camera number. (I suggest naming your cameras in the Modify tab, so that you know what's what.)

Experimenting with different kinds of cameras, and getting to know what kind of effects you can obtain with them, is pretty important in achieving some measure of complexity. For example, to adjust the type of lens from the default 35mm, simply select the Modify tab, choose your camera in the scene, and pick a new lens.

As with any program, but *especially* when you're modeling with Max, save often and incrementally, and backup everything. You *will* crash, and you *will* lose data. It's inevitable, but it is possible to minimize your losses.

Getting back to my techniques for manipulating some_flower2, having decided that it was suitable for my needs I deleted all the extra stuff in the file that I didn't want, and settled down to work with a single group of objects. Since most of the modeling was already complete, I simply added a few more duplicate pieces of existing structures (hold down SHIFT, and drag the object) and placed them as randomly as possible in relation to each other, to further the concept of chaos.

At this stage, as a way of getting as many different images of my object as I could comfortably deal with, I started rendering out animated sequences from all of the cameras, using a process that I'll describe here. First, I chose the Select and Rotate tool from the Main Toolbar tab, and selected the carefully modeled, 'useless' 3D objects. Then, I switched on the Animate button, and moved the timeline scrubber 4 frames along. Next, I rotated the object 180 degrees or so in the Front view port. Finally, I turned off Animate, and previewed my work by rendering out a few sequences.

Since the animation was a quick half-turn that lasted for only four or five frames, I was left with about 36 images to play with, after all the camera views had been rendered. Rendering is a fairly simple process, but it can be *extremely* time consuming. Furthermore, I was exporting sequences of images rather than QuickTime movies, so file management became very important here. For each camera, I created a separate folder, and then rendered PNG sequences. A rough outline of this procedure is as follows.

Go to Rendering > Render, and examine the Time Output section of the resulting dialog. Select Range, and enter the length of your animation. (As stated, mine was four frames long.) In the Output Size section, go for 800 x 600 pixels, or something even bigger if you wish.

In the Render Output segment, select Files, a file type (for stills, I prefer PNGs, because of the option to include an alpha channel or transparency, rather than a simple white background), and a file name (the name you choose here will have numbers appended to it for each frame of the animation). Finally, you can hit the Render button; if you've done everything correctly, you should have a sequence of images to view. Ah, the joys of 3D rendering.

My initial thought then was to randomly select a number out of a hat to discover which render to work with for the Photoshop portion of this project (more chaos!), but in the end I cheated and ended up using the one that I liked the most. I have that file listed in my notes as being named rhdtht.png, whatever that means. The reason that I chose to export short sequences was to maximize the possibility of getting a random picture that I might not have counted on taking. This again helped to address the theme of geometry and chaos working in concert.

At this point, I want to provide one last bit of instruction, because it describes an effect that I used on a few of the cameras. Over the course of my education in the use of 3ds max, I've had the luck to be exposed to some really talented 3D artists, and I just happened to be around when one such person discovered that it was possible to use the FFD 4x4x4 modifier on cameras and lights. Thanks, Patrick.

First, drop any 3D object you like into a scene. Then, take a camera of any type, and position it so that your object takes up the total field of view.

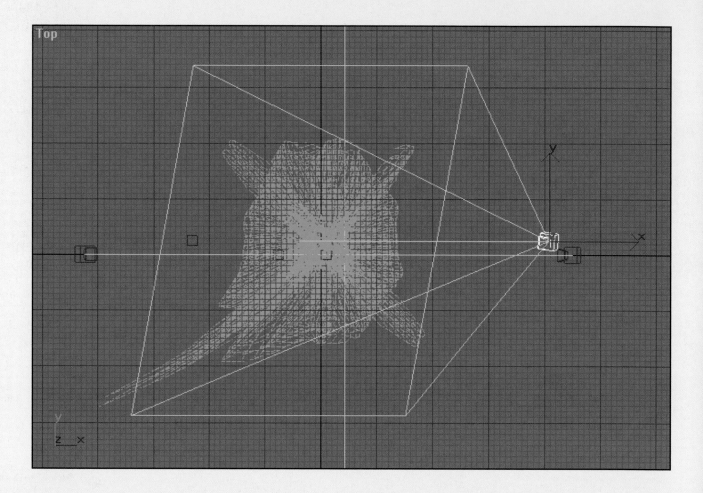

Now, with the camera selected, you can go to the Modify tab as before, choose the FFD 4x4x4 modifier, and get control of the control points. Then, choose the Select and Move tool from the Main Toolbar, and pull on the control points in any direction that you want. Choose whatever view you want, and experiment with the degrees to which you can distort the appearance of your object by manipulating the points on the camera. Note that initially, the control points will appear as a very tight group, so you may have to zoom right in on the object and play around until you grab the point that you want to affect.

The same methodology can be applied to any light, and by using the various FFD modifiers you can create all sorts of strange shadows.

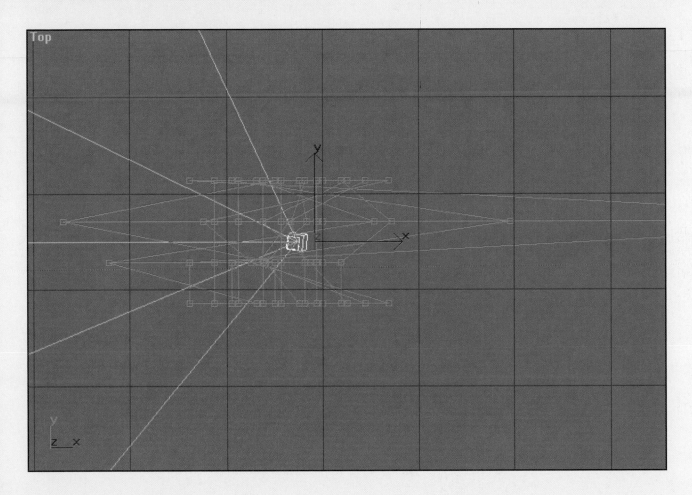

The render that I ended up using was not actually a result of this effect, but it's kind of fun nonetheless. `rhdtht.png` was simply a snapshot taken by the camera I had installed as a default viewer, and it just happened to capture that picture in one of the many animated sequences. I've stated and restated the theme and probably the title of this book a lot, and maybe I approached the assignment too literally, but I was fairly happy with the effect that was created in this portion of the development. The next step for me was to transfer the image files to my other computer, and to introduce the same concepts of *Geometry and Chaos* in a graphical environment: Photoshop.

Aesthetics of geometry versus aesthetics of chaos

working a theme to death... object... adjustment layers... pinning down chaos... 4 versions... tweaking the final product... fireworks... done

Construction-wise, my original plan of attack was to apply the same kind of "pull the numbers out a hat" approach that I'd considered using in 3ds max to whatever I was going to make in Photoshop. I would divide the canvas using a grid, and pull out numbers to determine the placement of the various elements. But just after I'd finished transferring the Max render, I decided that I wasn't going to take things that far. That was partly because I really liked this one shot, but mostly because I'm lazy, and in any case I wanted to pursue some ideas that I'd developed in some of the sketches I made during the concept development phase. I felt this picture was the strongest of the bunch.

My new plan was to simply roll with it: to place numerous copies of the same image on the canvas, and see where I ended up. I first created duplicates of the image, and sized them to the dimensions that I wanted with the Transform tool. By grouping a variety of these layers and then overlaying the images on top of each other, new shapes seemed to develop. In some instances, I flattened the 3D graphics by filling them with color, using the paint bucket tool.

The following sequence of images shows how this developed.

Once I'd reached the point where I liked the way the 3D elements were working together, I started placing large blocks of color over the top of the 3D work, in an effort to 'box in' and 'pin down' the imagery. This was the idea I expressed in my essay, and it still sounds pretty heavy, but I can't think of a better way of describing what I was trying to accomplish.

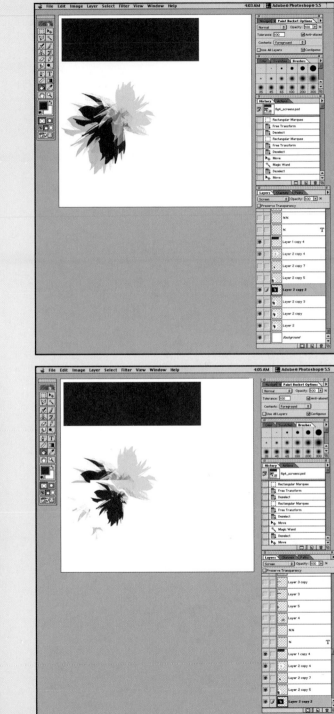

Using the basic shape of the objects as a pattern allowed me to cut out chunks from the heavy blocking that I was using. The Magic Wand was my weapon of choice at this point, and by selecting the filled 3D objects I was able to get a pattern with relatively sharp edges. Furthermore, by placing the cut out blocking in relation to the 3D work. I was able to get a nice 'punch out' effect that in turn created the illusion that there were more elements involved than there really were.

Over about two days, I went through a number of different basic layouts using similar methods, but with several different color variations – until eventually I arrived at four roughly finished pieces that I thought fit into my overall concept. You'll find finished versions of all four on the CD, and I like bits and pieces of all of them, but the one that I felt best accomplished what I had initially conceived was a file called geo_chaos2.psd. It did require a few basic text treatments to get it print-ready, but design-wise it was pretty much there. The other designs show a pretty steady progression towards the finished piece; the only real difference between them is the text treatment I transferred over from Fireworks.

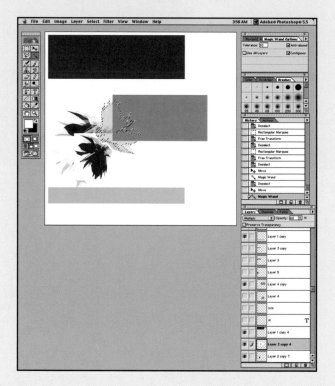

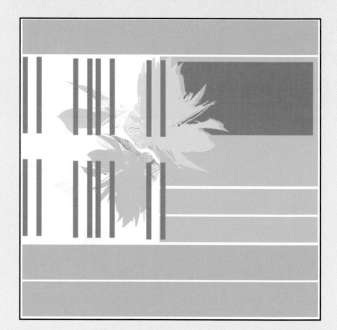

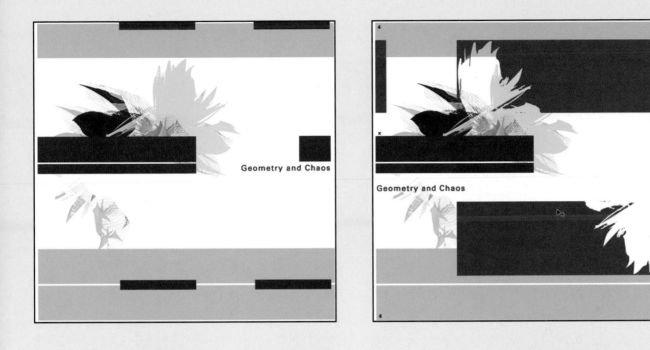

Fireworks is a brilliant design tool that I use quite a bit in my day-to-day web design work, and the facts that it's vector-based and optimized for web development make it indispensable. When compared to Photoshop, text created in Fireworks usually comes out crisper – it renders better on the Web, and in the few instances where I've used it to develop work for print. The Fireworks end of things was quite simple: I recreated the same preliminary kerning and font sizes, copied and pasted the new text graphics into the Photoshop file, and moved them into position. The final result of all my fiddling was a piece called *Geometry and Chaos*.

Conclusion

I haven't gone into any real detail about modeling techniques, or theories of graphic design, because I think that tutorials like that teach you someone else's habits. And all my habits are bad: I don't name my layers unless I'm forced to, I can never remember how I've done something five minutes after I've done it, I model in 3D without having concept sketches or a set plan, and I often have no clue what's going to end up sitting on my canvas at the end of the day.

That said, developing a concept and working the theme really helped to keep me on point, and I think that it shows in the results. Technically, what I've done is to try to outline a few aspects of a huge program, and to explain how I work through problems and approach segments of production with different forms of experimentation. The result of that experimentation is often a number of 'happy accidents' and unusual practices, but they work for me. I reconcile this with the knowledge that after a while, repetition turns these 'accidents' into techniques rather than flukes, demonstrating that that the learning process is still continuing.

Although the theme of chaos that I held onto over the course of this build has crept its way into every nook and cranny of the project, I hope that the hints, tips, and periods of instruction contained within this tutorial will be of service to you. It's been with a great deal of irony that I've applied knowledge that I considered quite useless in the past, to objects that often seen quite useless to me now, and ended up with something completely useful.

Outta here.

%

4

x

4

Individual:Deepseat.Net%Project:Four%Theme:Geometry%and%Chao

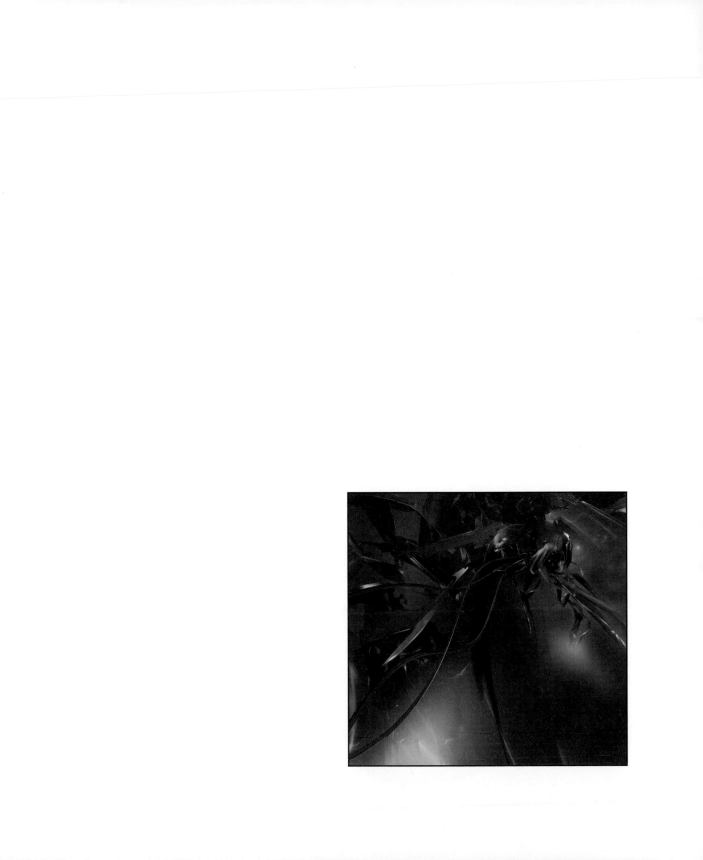

When I was younger, I never wanted to be a designer. I didn't even know what a designer was. The things that interested me were comics, toys, space, and video games. I would read through my comic books; I'd play with my Transformers and Lego bricks and build things; I'd look through a telescope and somehow recreate the universe in my mind; and I would destroy every video game I owned. All the time, though, I would wonder how these things were *made*, and I can remember the day when I decided that I would discover how to make things for myself. I guess you could say that from a very young age, I always wanted to be a creator.

Much later, in high school, a friend showed me a collage that he had made. I'd never known anyone who had created something like that before, and I was instantly hooked. I'd always pictured huge corporations spending months at a time creating the advertisements that I saw in magazines, or comics, or whatever. I hadn't realized that one person could do the same thing on their own. I got myself a computer, a copy of Adobe Photoshop... and that's where it all began. I'd sit back, listen to music, and jam.

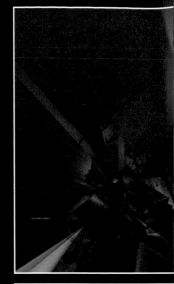

DISCLAIMER   SHOWCASE   PRODUCT   LIST   ABOUT   CONTACT

I actually don't like calling myself a designer. To me, 'design' sounds like you're solving problems, and although that can be fun, what I like most is to create digital art. If you want to use labels, I'd call myself a graphic artist, rather than a designer. Although I like and respect how things work, it's always the visual end product that I enjoy the most.

In the years since I first started designing, I've noticed a huge change in my work, and in my process. At first, I created minimal pieces – maybe a simple illustration or something in black and white with just a little type. Gradually, I started getting deeper into the work I was creating, adding more depth and emotion. Recently, clients have been asking for NGINCO-style work, which is excellent – I hope to get more clients like this!

DIGITAL THRENODY BY KONSTRUKTIV

NGINCO started out as a name behind my work, whatever it may have been. I coined it with the deliberate intention of it meaning nothing at all, because names like that have always interested me. (Take Sony, for instance: interesting word, interesting products.) It was born on May 1st, 2000.

ylocopa

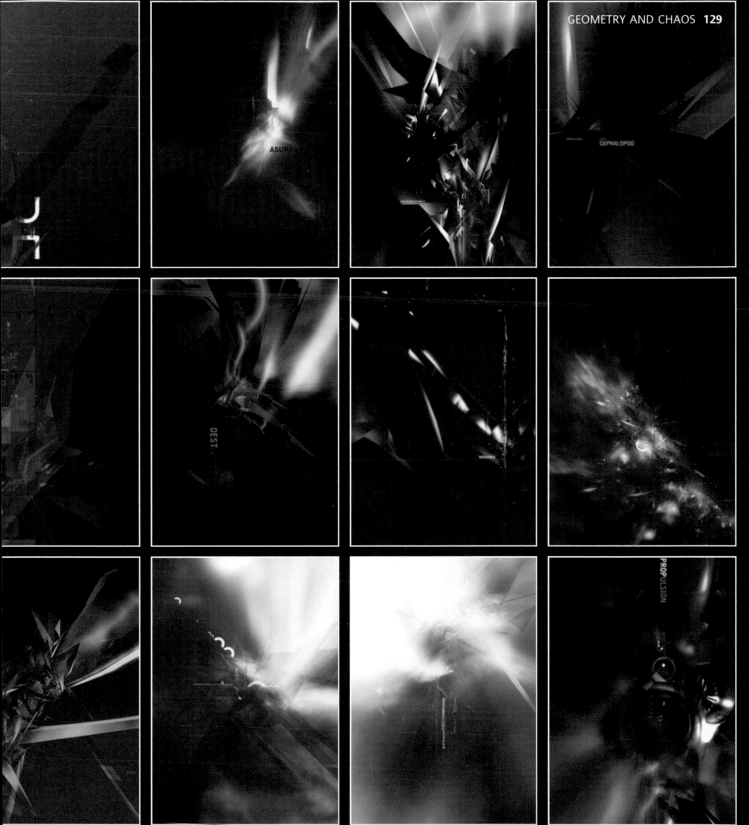

I can honestly say that I wouldn't be at the point I am now if it hadn't been for the amazing team I worked with at Vir2L in DC. Before I started there, I was doing client work that didn't push my creativity to any level other than satisfying the client. That's always the most important thing of course, but there's so much more you can do. When you can push boundaries, and break rules, and add your own style, it makes your work much more enjoyable. Vir2L was the time when my work became more 'art' than 'design'. There was such an amazing creative vibe there, full of inspiration and motivation, that it pushed me to new levels.

In the last year, I've learned above all that the most important thing is motivation. You'll get nowhere if you sit around doing nothing, or staring at a blank canvas trying to work it all out in your head. Throw stuff onto your canvas, give it some form, and build from there. When you start to see something forming, you're motivated to keep going.

For me, inspiration can come from anything, from video games, to New York, to anime, to music. I've been an avid gamer for a lot of years, and there's more inspiration to be found in this field than you might at first imagine – the way that some video games mix interactivity with special effects and movies is quite astonishing. New York contains enough inspiration to last a person a lifetime, and anime is stunning just because the artists create such crazy machinery, and use really great colors. The motivation I get from seeing other work, and different surroundings, gets me in the zone – and that's when I jam best.

But the most important source of inspiration is music. I listen to all kinds of stuff, ranging from heavy metal to reggae, through hip-hop, scratching, trip-hop, electronic, and evil orchestrated music. What I listen to almost forms what I'm doing, as though I'm not even working myself, but the music is controlling my mouse. It's strange, but it's all about the flow. When I was working on *Idiopathica*, for example, I listened to some heavy metal from a German band called Banished Reality who had contacted me earlier about designing a CD cover for them, some Pink Floyd, and some Philip Glass. Some people have been able to tell what music I listen to by looking at my work, and I find that pretty interesting.

A lot of people seem to ask whether I draw my pieces before I create them. I'd have to say that in most cases, I don't. Until recently, it had been a year or so since I touched a sketchpad – I'd been spending so much time in front of a computer that I hadn't really looked to using pen and paper. Now, though, I *am* just getting back into some doodling and drawing. I think it's a good thing to do, and it definitely expands your imagination. I've always been into graffiti, and a lot of the things I draw have that kind of feel: funky lines and things that intertwine.

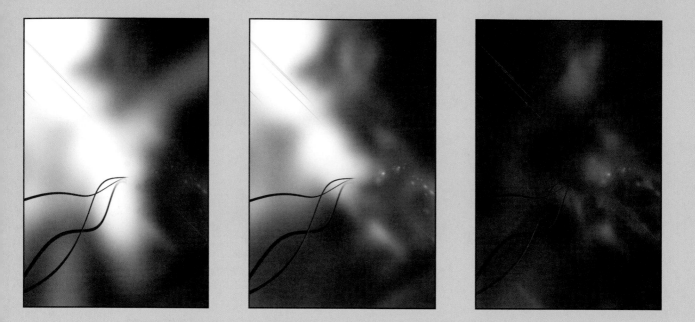

When friends of ED first contacted me, and said that this book was going to be based around *Geometry and Chaos*, my first reaction was to want to create something very detailed, something very flat, and something very broken. After a little thought, however, I decided that this would be too obvious, and I wanted to do something a little different. I'd unite chaos and geometry in a structured form – only not.

Before I start a project, I tend to have a vague idea of what I'm going to do, but I never know exactly how it will end up. For me, having an exact idea robs you of the chance to experiment, and that can be boring. From the beginning of *this* project, I knew that I wanted to create something that was a change from what I normally do. My previous pieces have contained mostly muted colors, with maybe a few brighter colors on top; they've tended to be very dark, with sharp shapes. I decided to try creating something with more colors, and a more 'alive' feeling to it. Also, I wanted to create something sci-fi, with a bit of an oriental feeling.

As well as the music I was listening to, particular inspiration for the piece came from video games. I've always enjoyed RPGs, and most recently I've been playing *Final Fantasy 9* on the PlayStation. The attention to detail that goes into the character design in all of SquareSoft's games is incredible, and there are a number in that game that made me decide it would be a good idea to create some sort of weird creature, in a weird space.

The process of creating *Idiopathica* was an interesting one. I worked several times on a few different ideas, but none seemed to be heading in the direction I wanted to go. As a result, I decided that I was going about it all wrong, and began modeling something in 3D first. This was a very experimental process — again, I started over several times, trying to get the look I was going for. It wasn't until the fourth try that I knew I was finally going in the right direction. Something about the colors I was working with, and the way my objects were forming, told me that it was starting to come together.

After I'd spent many hours building the 3D model, it was time to go into Photoshop. As happens so often, when I started jamming, I quickly realized that the positions of the elements in my renders were not exactly where I wanted them to be — so I changed them. Once I'm in Photoshop, there are no specific techniques, or any particular order, in which I work. Like anyone else, I do what feels right for the piece I'm working on.

I'm not entirely sure what my co-authors will do with this piece, but I can't wait to see – the overall reaction to the theme was an extremely positive one from everyone involved. I'm familiar with most of their work, and it will be interesting to see where they take this objective. I have a feeling that most will be abstract, but there's really no telling what everyone will do.

When I look at *Idiopathica*, it seems almost like a drawing, or a painting. In fact, when I showed it to a friend, that's the first thing he said. It certainly didn't turn out how I'd first pictured it, and writing the tutorial was quite difficult because so much experimentation was involved. There was a lot of movement back and forth, and I didn't take any screenshots during the whole process. There was no preordained way of creating a certain effect, or creating a certain thing. If you don't experiment, you don't push yourself.

When the piece was complete, I would say that I had accomplished my first goal: more colorful, more alive, and sci-fi. It was nice to create something a bit different, but still the same. The interesting thing about this piece, and I think why it will fit well in this book, is because everyone who has seen it has seen something *different* in it.

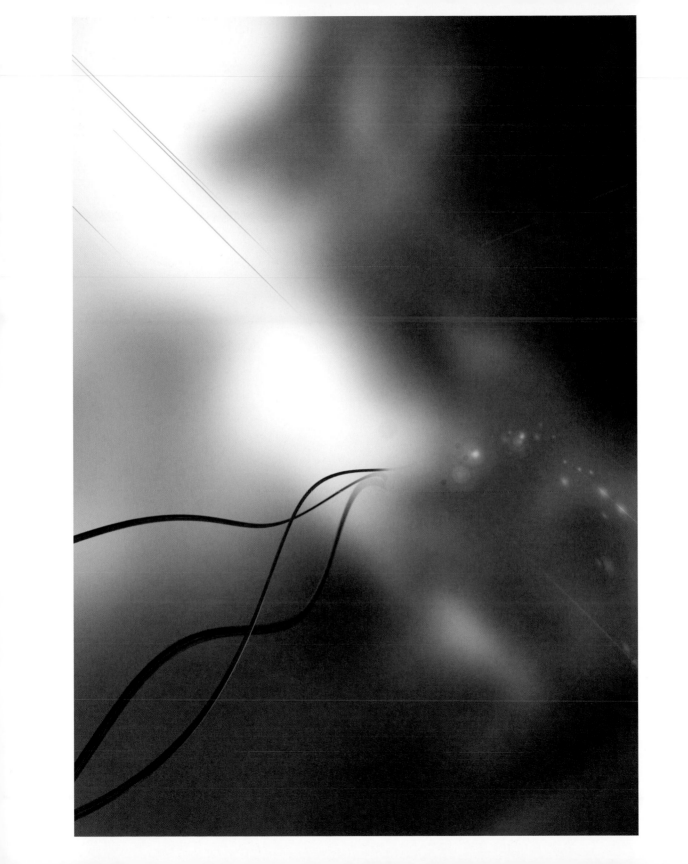

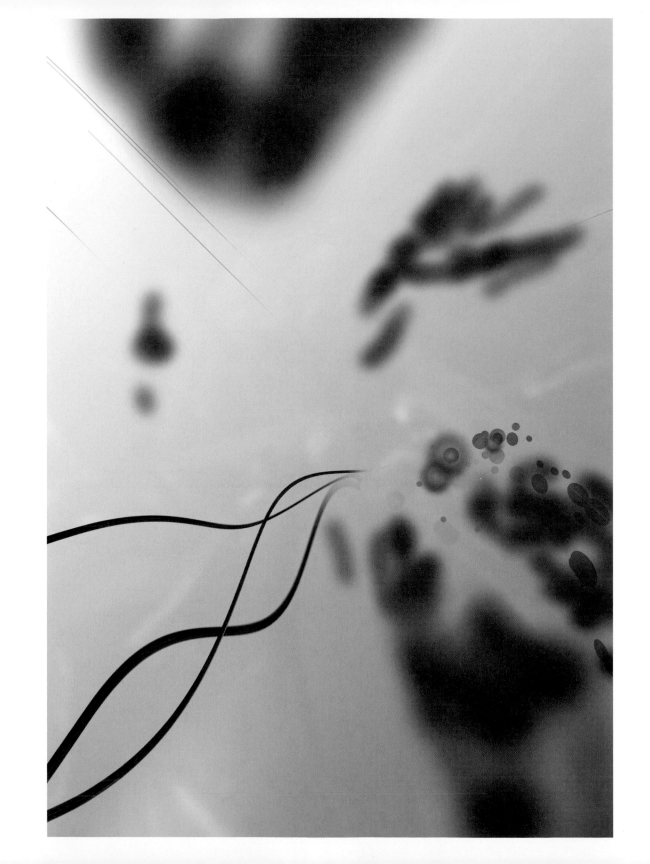

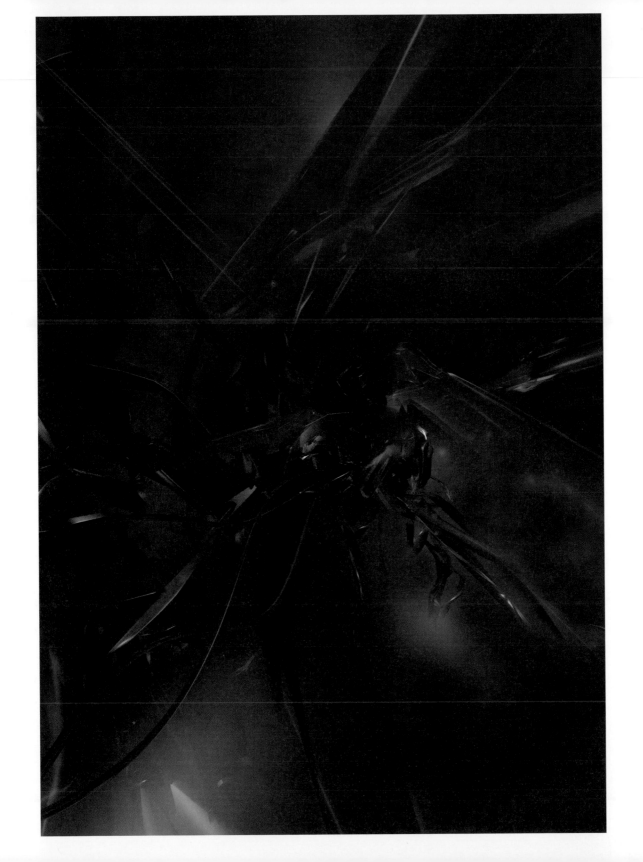

This piece – *any* piece – would not have been possible without hours of experimentation with light, color, composition, and shape. There really is no set way of creating a full piece – as this book surely demonstrates, different people do things in different ways, and in a different order – but allow this tutorial to be a guide to my personal method. With that in mind, let's turn on some music and begin.

What I'm about to explain is the creation process behind my piece for this book, *Idiopathica*, from the background to the foreground. Because so much of the way I work comes down to intuition, there are places in the process where it was very difficult to explain exactly what's going on; where that happens, I've tried to describe my thoughts, and to explain a means by which you might go about doing something similar.

When I first start a project, I find it easiest to begin with the background, and then to build forward. There are periods during the compositing process, however, when things are moved around significantly – sometimes, some of your foreground pieces will end up as part of the background. This can create a sense of depth, and it's great to experiment with.

To create a background for a piece like *Idiopathica*, there are several techniques that it's useful to have at your disposal. First of all, I believe that you should become completely comfortable with using Photoshop's Airbrush tool – for me, it's the most important in the box. When you're practicing with the airbrush, try different brush sizes, all the way from 1 to 999. Of course, depending on your goals, some will prove to be more useful than others, but it's vital to have a feel for which brushes are best for what use. In this piece, for example, I was mostly using size 600 and size 999 brushes.

Similarly, there's no set of rules I can give you that governs what softness or spacing to use in every case – it all depends on what you're trying to achieve. If you're working with something big, it's best to start by using big brush sizes, then shrinking down – but you're not always going to be working in the same dimensions, at the same DPI, or with the same elements, so it's impossible to give firm guidance. The Airbrush tool is important precisely because it's so versatile, and allows for so much experimentation.

Predictably, then, the background you can see above was created entirely using the airbrush – I just selected the tool (999 brush size, 50% opacity), and started coloring. Once I was satisfied, I continued with another color that blended with the previous one. It can be helpful to pretend that you're creating an airbrush painting, using big brushes for the general shape, and switching to smaller brushes to provide definition. The key thing to remember is that when you're creating a background, it doesn't have to be very detailed, or even very structured. If you need to, you can always go back to those aspects later on.

Although it's superficially fairly simple, the process of creating a background by this method can be quite time consuming. There are some shortcuts that you can use to accelerate matters, but remember that if you rush something, the chances are that the end result won't be as good as it could have been. A technique that I've used on occasion is to take a photo, select a part of it, scale it up, and then apply a blur to it. If you want to attempt this, try to find a shot that displays interesting lighting, and use that area as your subject for enlargement.

With the background in a state that I was essentially happy with, the logical next step was to create the foreground. From the beginning, I had planned to create something with a sci-fi theme, so I decided that it was time to launch Discreet's 3ds max, and see what would form.

I started by using the line tool to make some simple shapes. Once I had those, I extruded them, deleted some parts of them, moved points around by editing the mesh... anything to create a structure that showed promise and would be interesting to work with. I gave the structure more definition by adding shapes, moving different points, duplicating, scaling, etc. There's a lot of experimentation that goes into creating abstract pieces in 3ds max, and no simple, set way of doing things.

Next, I opened up the Material Editor and started creating some color schemes. To do this, I modified the default color (gray) to my liking by changing the Ambient and Diffuse settings, and altered a number of the other parameters in the dialog box. This process took a while for the simple reason that I experimented with many colors, but I ended up with what you see here.

Once I'd assigned my 'new' materials to the shapes I wanted them on, I created a Target Camera and moved it around until I was pleased with the position and framing of the structure.

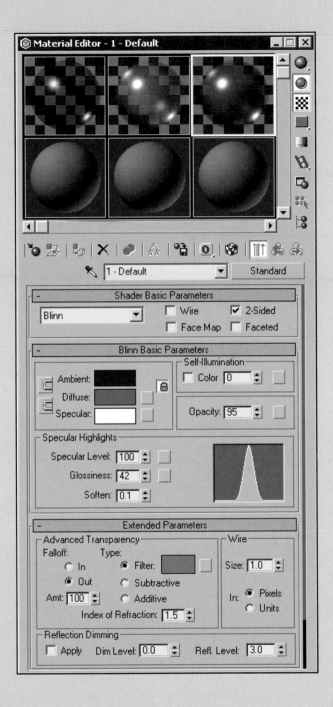

When you're working in 3ds max, it's a good idea to add a light source, to give your objects a more realistic feel. Using a Target Spotlight can create a less flat-looking surface, and it's really great to experiment in order to generate different effects.

> When you use lights, it's worth remembering that the closer you place one to your object, the *darker* most of the object will be. This is because the light needs some distance to 'spread out' and provide more even illumination. Move your light away from your object, and you'll start to see it act as a 'better' source.

At this stage, it was time to render. I changed none of the default options, but I did use a very big size (6000 x 4500 pixels), because I knew that I was making something for print. Actually, unless you've got a particular goal in mind,

you tend *always* to want to work at the biggest size you can, because it's much easier to scale down than to scale up when you're working with your render in Photoshop. I always save my renders as Targa (TGA) files, because they enable you to select the alpha channel in Photoshop, making the removal of the background a simple matter.

The two screenshots below show renders of the same model from two different perspectives. In fact, I make sure to produce several renders whenever I create something in 3ds max, because more often than not they prove to be useful. Of course, you can always go back and move around the camera or the lights to create new renders, but I find that having a decent selection to start with is a good way of kick-starting my creativity. For this piece, two renders were enough, and it was time to switch applications.

This section of the tutorial includes numerous images of the Photoshop user interface. As new layers are added to the composition, I've highlighted them in a light blue color.

When I got into Photoshop, I realized that I didn't actually want to use all of the background that I'd made when I started — it didn't seem to fit too well with the renders that I'd made in Max. For the first step in this process,

then, I created a layer called bg - solid that contained just a vertical linear gradient, from dark to a little lighter. The lighter side was then placed at the top of the piece.

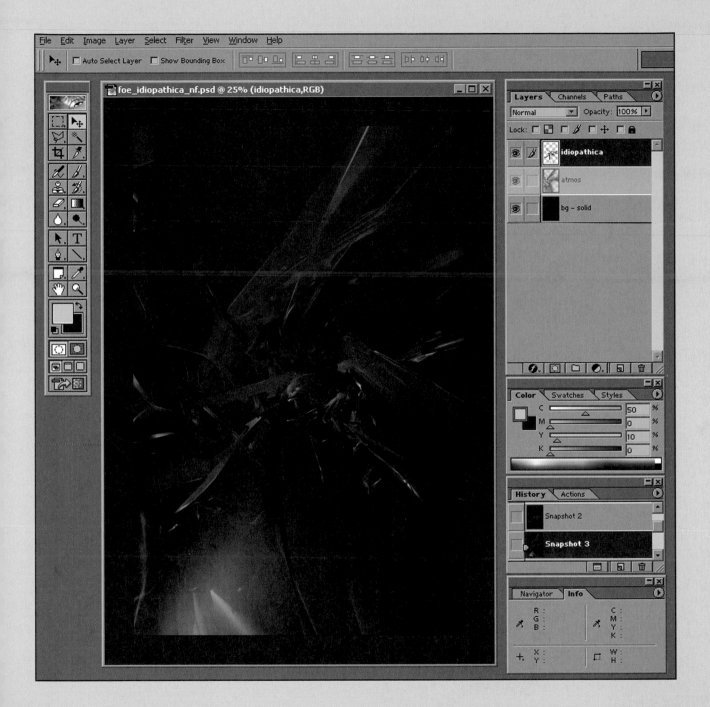

I then superimposed my renders by placing them into layers named idiopathica and atmos, and used the Eraser tool – with the mode set to Airbrush – to remove parts of them, in order to make them blend better. Depending on the area I was trying to erase, I used several different brush sizes – when you're performing this kind of operation, it's completely up to you to choose a size that's right for the task.

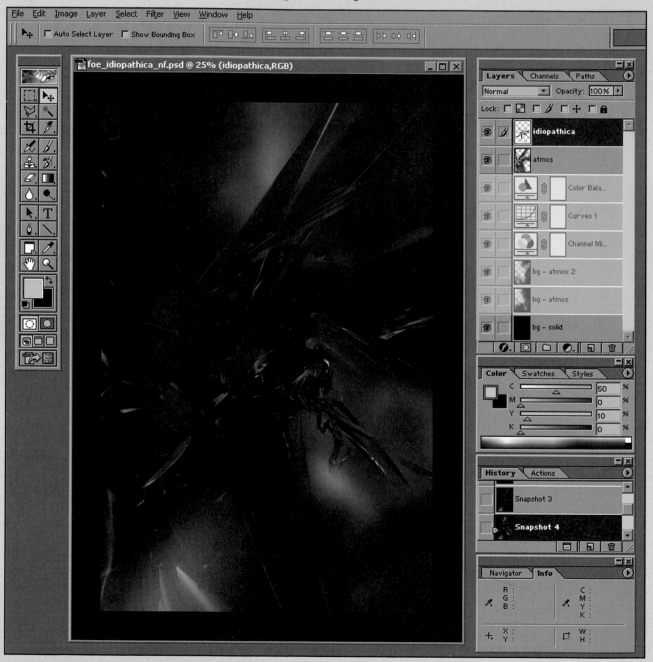

After doing that, I thought that I should test out the background I'd made previously, by placing it beneath the renders. To add more light still, I decided to duplicate the layer and apply the Screen blending mode, creating two new layers called bg - atmos and bg - atmos 2. On doing this, however, I discovered that the original color of my background didn't go well with the renders at all, so I adjusted the colors with first the Channel Mixer, then Curves, and finally Color Balance. The precise settings for these are given in the following dialog boxes.

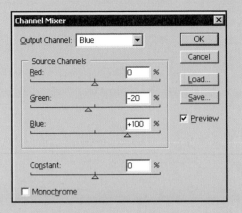

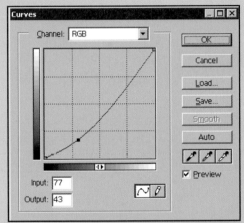

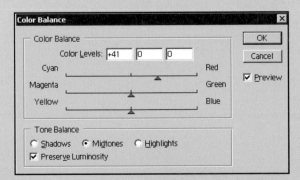

Now that the background and the renders matched up nicely, I decided to add just a little more red to the overall color of the piece, so I placed another Color Balance layer at the top of the current layer stack. I raised the red level by 50 points in the Midtones, added a gradient mask, and reduced the opacity to 50% so that the red wasn't overpowering.

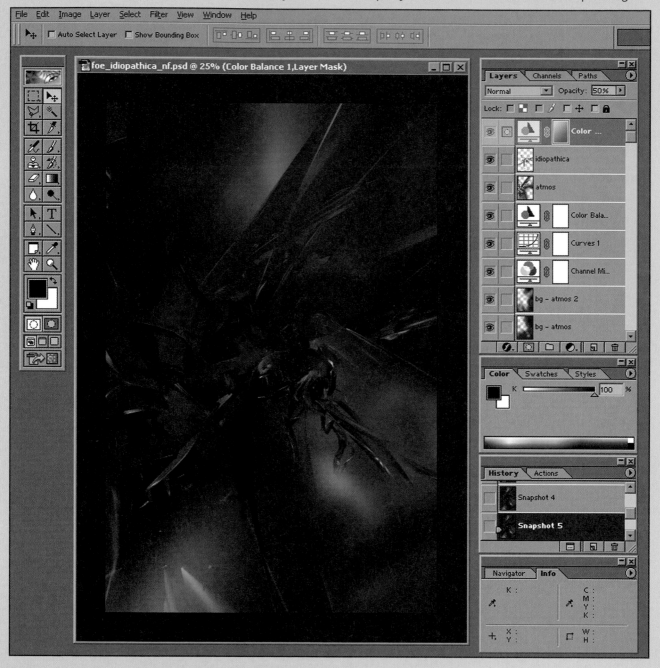

I was now pleased with the overall composition and its colors, so it was time to fine-tune the piece by adding details and a few other features. After looking over the piece for a while, I decided to build some elements around the main structure. I started by taking the Airbrush and making a circle with a smaller, lighter circle inside. I duplicated this circle a few times, scaled them all down, and placed them 'beneath' the airbrushed background. I repeated this process with several other circles; the first of the two screenshots below has the other layers hidden, while the second has all layers visible.

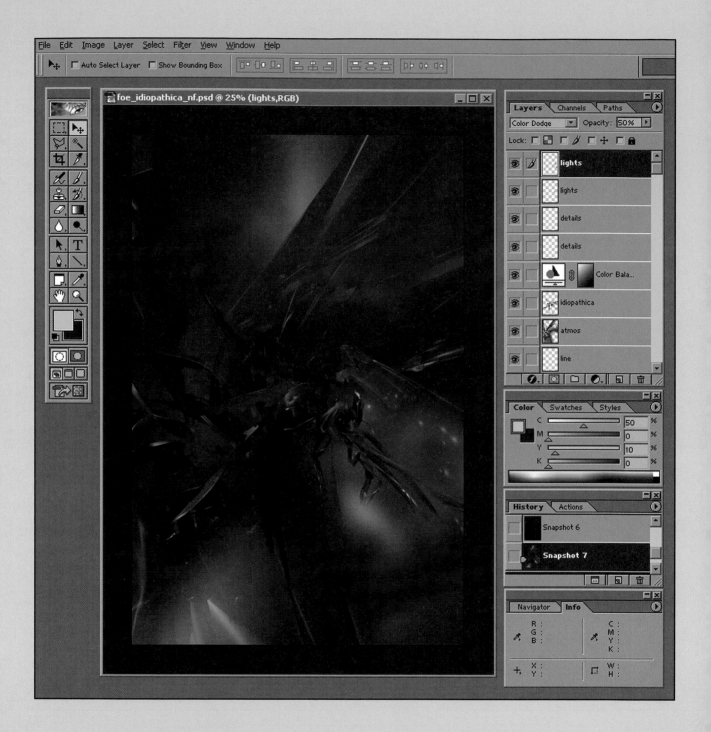

Despite its most recent additions, I decided that the piece still needed some more fine details, so I continued on, adding lines and 'vines'. The former, predictably, were created using the Line tool, while the latter involved the Pen tool to start with, before the resultant paths were stroked with a size-5 airbrush. Even then, the vines were too big at first, so I scaled them down.

After that, I duplicated the line layers, blurred the duplicates, and lightened them just a little bit by using Hue/Saturation to produce a 'glowing' effect.

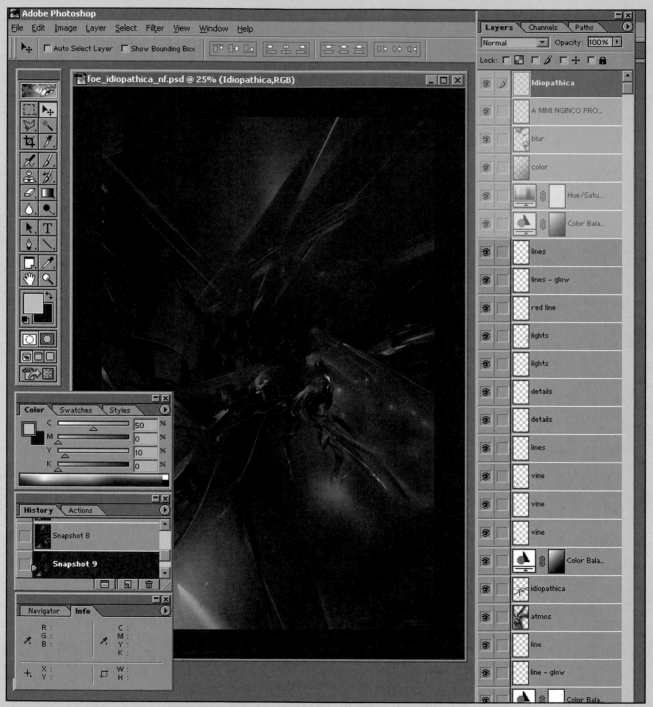

The final steps were then simply to clean up anything I didn't like, and to blur any 'bad' parts of the image. When you're working with the Airbrush, you'll often find that it creates 'fragments'; to clear these out, I use the Blur tool. I also added a last pair of adjustment layers, because I felt that the image was *too* bright, and I wanted it to be a little more muted. Those settings were as below.

The very last step of all was to add my title, which is tiny and sits at the bottom right of the image...

...and there you have it. Although this tutorial hasn't been a step-by-step guide (I hope you'll agree that there's no way it could have been), I trust that it's helped you to understand the process of mixing 3D chaos with Photoshop to create an abstract piece. I hope too that it might inspire you to try something comparable for yourself.

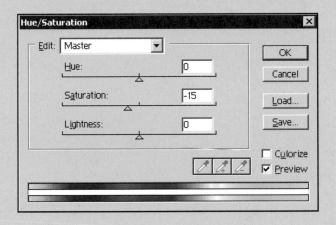

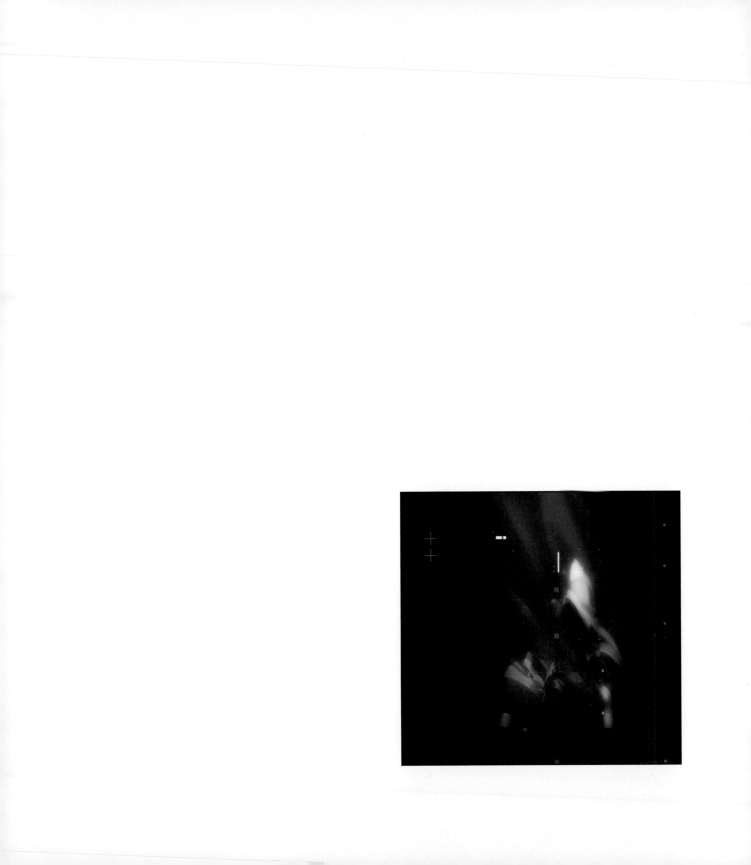

My work, and how and why I design, isn't easy to put into linear writing. Most of the ideas, and the stuff I do, come and go on a whim. Everything we do is influenced by our surroundings, and most of my ideas come to me from having long talks with friends, or going for a walk in downtown London. Just walking, looking at buildings and people, and reading signs in the streetscape... maybe a word or a slogan will catch my eye and give me an idea. But it's mostly just the walking that does it – it clears your head and lets your mind run free.

Sometimes, I get the feeling of having come full circle. Back in college, you could do whatever you wanted (as long as your professors agreed with it), and pretty quickly I became obsessed with my Mac. Everything I did had to go through Photoshop – I knew every filter by heart, and I was more than glad to show it. Then I graduated and started working... it was goodbye to the fancy designs, and hello to the corporate way of life and web design:

1. Keep your file size as low as you can
2. Keep it nice and clean
3. No fancy graphics, because the client might not get it
4. Think about structure, usability, and communication
5. Don't use Flash; the client doesn't want his users to depend on plug-ins
6. Form follows function

You get my drift, and it's not that these are all bad things – true, it would be fun just to lash out and give big corporate machines like Honeywell or Ricoh a site that blasted off the screen, but that would be the easy way out. Instead, you have to come up with a design that does all the things listed before, works on every platform and browser possible, and still looks good. And you have to retool your thinking process along the way.

After two years of the corporate machine, and doing some fun stuff on the side, I'd had enough and wanted something else... and that was to go to London and start working at the London branch of Vir2L. It was great to go to work at a company where everyone was equally excited about design, and where you could talk to someone about it, and they would understand. It was also great that the programmers, instead of going on about why Star Trek: The Next Generation was superior to the original series, dug the same stuff that we did.

Everything had turned around: here, you could design stuff how you wanted it. Sure, you had to keep in mind the list of dos and don'ts, but you could go wild as well. I still like putting together 'corporate' stuff, nice and tight, but I can play around a lot more too.

I've always found inspiration from my friends and the people I work with – I like to call it 'friendly competition'. Some of my best friends in Belgium still make me feel small and leave me in awe when I see their work. The same goes for the period when I worked at Vir2L. When you're spending 10 to 12 hours a day, 24/7, in the same space as people who are at least as driven and obsessed by what they do as you are, it's bound to rub off on you.

For example, just before I came to London, I was making plans and starting to map out what was eventually going to become www.ximeralabs.com – but there was no hurry... it would be finished when I felt like it. At Vir2L, however, I was confronted with a bunch of guys who all had their own sites up and running, and put the heat on me to be online too. That was motivation – sure, it's all done for the love of the game, but you still end up spending days and nights working on your stuff. In a way, it's a representation of who and what you are.

The weird thing is, when I'm working on something for a client, it 'clicks' straight away. I know exactly what I'm going to do, and what it's going to look like. When I'm working for myself – or on anything to which my name will be attached – I get some kind of block, and it takes ages before I can force something out of my machine that I can get along with. Putting my site together, for example, took around ten months (and about a truckload of cigarettes and coffee) before I was happy with my stuff. And stranger still, no matter how many times you try, the first idea is almost always the best one.

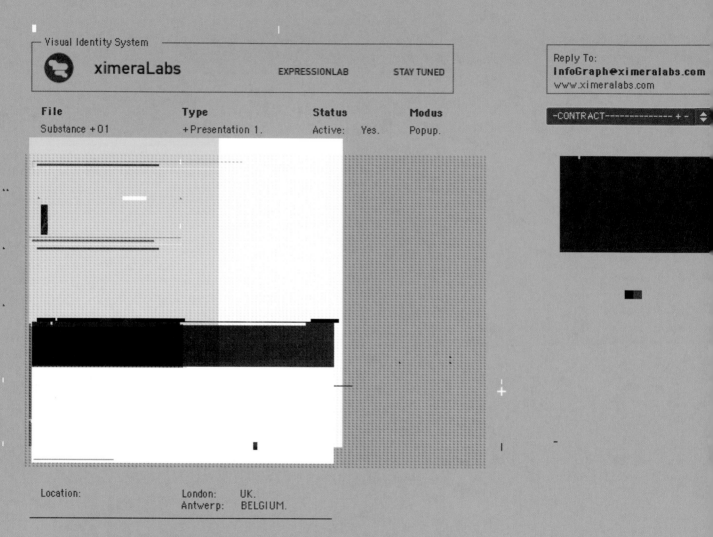

Visual Identity System

ximeraLabs   EXPRESSIONLAB   STAY TUNED

File	Type	Status		Modus
Substance +01	+Presentation 1.	Active:	Yes.	Popup.

Reply To:
InfoGraph@ximeralabs.com
www.ximeralabs.com

-CONTRACT-------------- + -

Location:	London:	UK.
	Antwerp:	BELGIUM.

Copyright © 2000-2001 www.ximeralabs.com | ximeraLabs

When I'd started thinking about what I wanted to put online, the first things that popped into my head were experimentation and expression: I wanted to express my own views and interests about design. At the time I didn't have a name for my site, but thanks to An, my then girlfriend, I got one: Chimera (in fact, Ximera), which means, "An illusion or fabrication of the mind." Yes! This was a perfect description of what I wanted to do – after all, everything we design is at first a figment of our imagination.

CHIMERA   AN ILLUSION OR FABRICATION OF THE MIND – UNREALIZABLE DREAM.
              AN INDIVIDUAL, ORGAN OR PART CONSISTING OF TISSUES OF DIVERSE GENETIC CONSTITUTION.
XIMERA   XIMERA(LABS) IS AN ONGOING PLATFORM FOR DIFFERENT DESIGN/WEB PROJECTS BECAUSE
INSPIRATION NEVER STOPS.
YOUR BEST IDEA IS NEVER GOOD ENOUGH. TECHNOLOGY KEEPS EVOLVING.

EXPAND – EXPERIENCE – SUBMERGE

Part of the reason why it then took ten months is that new ideas distract me far too easily. Suddenly, I just had to have a scrolling news service on my site. Then, I found some cool Flash scripts, so I wanted to do something super-interactive. Before that, I'd modeled a robot, and the whole site was going to be some sort of fake concept/product site centered on that idea. And then there were my flirtations with Shockwave and QuickTime (or was that before the Flash part?). The only thing that didn't change over time was my logo; that was right straight away, apparently.

Anyway, there eventually came a point where I'd started over for what seemed like the hundredth time, and I came up with a design that I liked! And instead of making new stuff and fleshing the whole thing out, I stayed with it. By accident, I cut up the design in Flash (Yes! Sometimes dumb luck can get you somewhere!), and rather than fixing it, I kept going, and started to resample it again and again. I liked this: seeing how far you could go with just one idea/design, and remixing it to get something new. If you go to my site and click on Presentation 1, you'll see what I've done: I just put one remix after the next, so that you get a static sequence with all the different variants of the image. In the end, I'd dropped all those great new ideas to go all the way back to square one: express yourself.

That's the story behind the site as it is right now, and I have to say that I'm happy with it. In this past year alone, I can see significant evolution in my style, and in my way of thinking about and approaching things. Why? I don't know. Probably because I've been working with a lot of likeminded people, exchanging ideas, working together on things... you know.

Right now, I'm hard at work on a big site update for ximeraLabs – and once again, it's going to be totally different from the stuff I've done before. I'm about halfway through Jeffrey Veen's The Art & Science of Web Design, which dives behind the scenes of web design to explain why the Web is as it is, and why there are all those things we have to take into account when designing for it. I was already well underway with the new design, but reading this book has made me think about starting over, going back to basics, and making my site as 'corporate' as I can. I'll apply all the rules of a 'good' corporate site to my own design aesthetics, and see what the result is.

Of course, in two weeks I'll read about, say, visual design systems for electric power grids, and try to incorporate that into my design too… and then it'll be next Christmas before the site sees the light of day! You're your own worst client: you want to have the best, but you want it fast. And you want to get it out of the way, so that you can start working on the next big thing you've been thinking about for the last month.

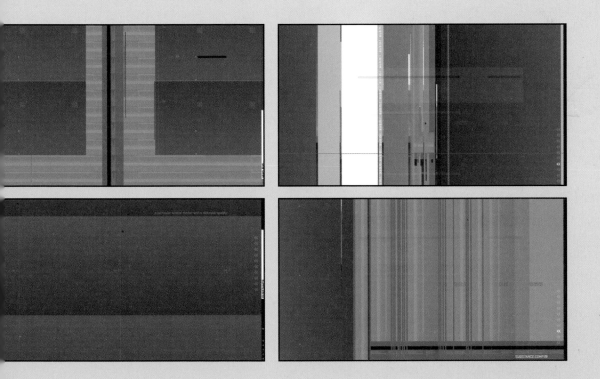

XIMERAlabs

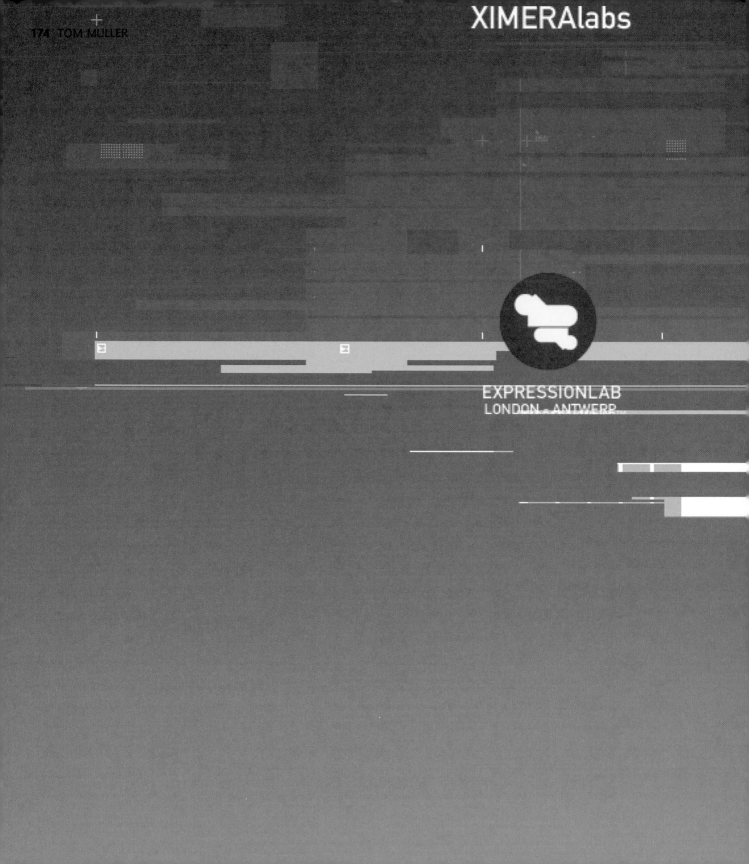

EXPRESSIONLAB
LONDON · ANTWERP

It's been said that in the early days of the Net, a lot of web designers tried to apply the rules and design outlook they brought with them from their experience of the printed page. My design education too focused mainly on print – back then, multimedia was a new thing, and didn't get much attention in school. But it was there nonetheless, and it had possibilities beyond your wildest dreams: you could actually animate your designs, add sound to them, build navigation systems...

What happened was that you, as new kid on the block, tried to go to the limit of those possibilities. You'd throw everything that you learned in print overboard, do wild things, and get away with it because it was multimedia: you had to think differently. And people would accept that because it was new, and they didn't have a clue. For me, 3D imagery was part of that whole, "It's a new medium and anything goes," thing. Using 3D wasn't new when I started out (there was already plenty of 3D design and illustration going on in print), but now multimedia and motion graphics were there to animate it.

My first foray into the world of 3D (and subsequently into the world of motion graphics) was pretty limited. All it entailed were small animations and 3D objects that I produced mainly for corporate clients – intro movies on CD-ROMs, the occasional splash page on a site, that kind of thing. And the stuff I modeled wasn't complex at all: animated logos, pie charts, simplified fax machines... the list goes on.

Later, when I got more confident with using 3D software, the experimentation began. Instead of modeling real (albeit simplified) objects, I started to create abstract images (like the one I did for this book, but much more rudimentary). For me, this was far more interesting – I was free to play with form, composition, and lighting effects. Occasionally, I still try my hand at modeling real-life objects, but it's ten times harder than just pulling and tweaking at a volume that's totally abstract.

Even now, I don't actually consider myself to be a fully-fledged 3D artist. Sure, I know how to use 3D programs, and I like to create 3D images, but most of the time we're talking about abstract imagery – weird shapes and forms without any real message or function. I tend not to use 3D as a main item in my personal work (but never say never); I like 2D as much – maybe even more – and I like to play around with layout too.

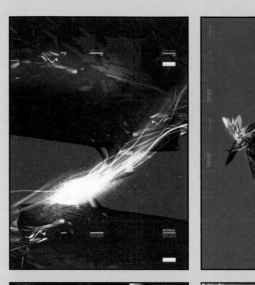

Geometry and Chaos... I have absolutely no clue how to start. Actually, that's not true – I've got too many clues. The possibilities are endless, and I don't know in what direction I should go. In a weird kind of way, the theme defines my thinking process: I'm a very structured person, but once I start tinkering on my machine, chaos ensues... until I eventually come up with something structured again.

I just finished a series of 3D images for Digital Vision, an online provider of stock images (www.digitalvisiononline.com). For that project, I created a single 3D image that served as a foundation, and then added huge amounts of detail and lighting until something very 'dense' emerged. When I started on the work for this book, my initial response was to create something similar, but I quickly left the idea behind: I'd just done stuff like that, and quite apart from the fact that it wouldn't really be challenging, it wouldn't fit the brief of the project. Certainly, I'd apply some of the same techniques in order to create the image, but the design philosophy behind it should be different.

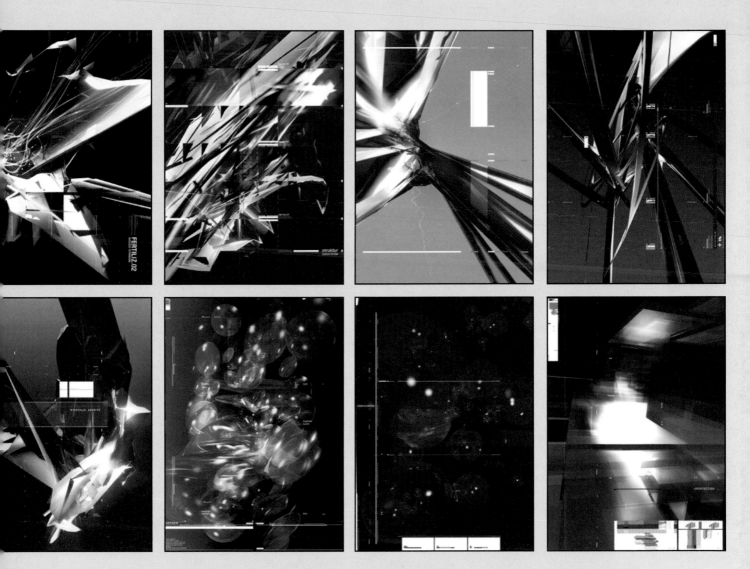

Something I knew from the start was that I didn't want to go 'hyper-layered'. I wanted to keep this piece as tight and clean as possible, and use a lot of white. (I like white: it's the cleanest color, and the basis of everything.) So here I am, sitting at home, watching TV and reading some comics, thinking about the stuff I want to do.

I think I want to turn the theme on its ear. Geometry and Chaos can mean anything – geometry can be chaos, and vice versa, and neither has to mean something that's visually complicated. Chaos can also be nothingness, and even complex geometry can look very simple at first sight. (Look at physics: a one-line equation can describe the most complex things in the universe.)

After a few days, I start: I know what concept I want to convey. I'm going to play around with the idea of putting two seemingly unrelated elements next to each other, so that you get a tension between them – a contrast between light and dark, if you will. Also, putting unrelated things next to each other creates a sort of chaos, because you don't know at first what to make of it. Only after looking at it for a bit longer do you start to see a relationship between the two. As for the 3D part... we'll see what comes out of the machine. The thing is, when you do things like designing abstract 3D forms and shapes, there is no set plan. You have an idea in the back of your head, but once you start actually constructing it, the chance factor takes over, and you let the design lead its own life. Your role becomes one of helping it along by turning the thing around, trying out different angles, etc. This can take a lot of time, and (in my case) a lot of cigarettes.

Render... look at the screen, staring at the image I just made.... kick back in my chair with a smoke... go back to the model and tweak it a bit... render... look at the screen, staring at the image I just made... kick back in my chair with a smoke... go back to the model and tweak it a bit... render... look at the screen, staring at the image I just made... kick back in my chair with a smoke...

So far, nothing concrete has actually happened. I still haven't made up my mind about the 3D image, but I'm not too worried about that. It's the part that comes after the modeling that's going to define the final look and feel of the piece. Anyway, it's anime night on the sci-fi channel, so at midnight I change from one screen to the other to watch big robots battling it out for a couple of hours. At 2am, fueled by the stuff on the TV, I start again. At 5am, I call it quits and go to bed.

After a couple of days of working like this, I come up with a model that I like: a kind of floating construction built from cylinders that (I think) looks like some kind of building. It doesn't say Geometry and Chaos to me at first sight, but I like the look and the dynamics of it, so I start rendering. At this stage, I open Photoshop: it's time to start working on the real thing.

What I do now is described in the tutorial; why I do it is rather harder to explain. What it comes down to is, "It feels and looks right." One way or another, I think that everything in design boils down to this point, whether you're designing a web site, a poster, a book, or whatever. Even after taking into account all the restrictions, and the dos and don'ts, you're still led by your gut instinct – and you can't teach that, because it's different for everyone. One person will stop at point X, while another will have to go to point Z before they're satisfied.

I'm the kind of person who goes all the way to point Z, and then back up again. I think it's better to do too much at first, even though it looks like crap from time to time. You never know until you've tried it. On this occasion, I decide to go for a double-page spread with the 3D element on one side, and nothing – or at least, almost nothing – on the other. It's easy to fill up a whole page; it's much harder to know exactly where to plant a small line or a splash of color, and not mess up the balance of the whole layout.

Somewhere in the middle of this process, I start thinking about *Complexity* and Chaos. I don't know why that happened; it's probably because I misread the title at first, and that got stuck in my mind. When it dawned on me that I was starting to go in a different direction, I panicked a little... but then just left it alone. I liked the idea of switching those words – it opened up a whole new perspective on the thing, and looked at the right way, both elements (the 3D design, and its big white space counterpart) could be considered as geometrical. Or even the whole layout, where you can find elements of the one in the other.

I start to think that it's actually quite funny to be working around this theme, and to have a big white space with only some colors on it next to a 3D element that at first sight has nothing to do with it. But in my opinion, it's the contrast and the interplay of the different elements that make it interesting. The colors themselves were decided as I went along: a cold bluish tone contrasting with a bright, dark orange.

At this point, I feel satisfied with the decisions I've made... but what are my collaborators coming up with? I know that they're all extremely talented, and they know their 3D, and it's not that I'm worried that my work will suffer by comparison... I'm just extremely curious to see their takes on the subject, and the approaches that I didn't think of. I've actually been chatting on ICQ with Nathan – him in New York, me in London – about the book, and the funny thing was, we didn't realize at first that we were working on the same thing! When we finally worked that out, my excitement only grew – it's always cool to work with someone who you appreciate and respect as an artist/designer.

Eventually, the double page spread is finished, but I feel that something's lacking. Maybe it's too little: on the left you have the 3D element, and on the right side just a white page with some graphics. I go back into it and start on a new design that goes before the spread – a sort of introduction, if you want – in which all the elements are presented partially in a new composition, but with the same philosophy behind it.

When both pieces are finished, I light up a smoke, and stare at my monitor for a few minutes. I decide to leave it alone. A little later, I remember that David Carson signed my copy of his book, 2nd sight: grafik design after the end of print, with the words:

2: Tom: keep designing 21/10/97

Yes, I will.

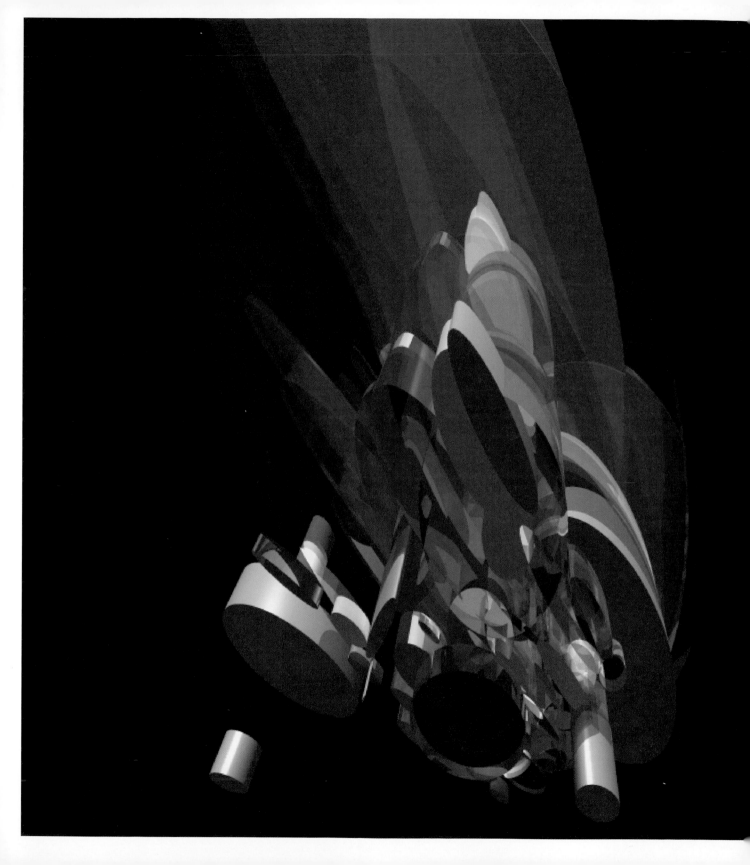

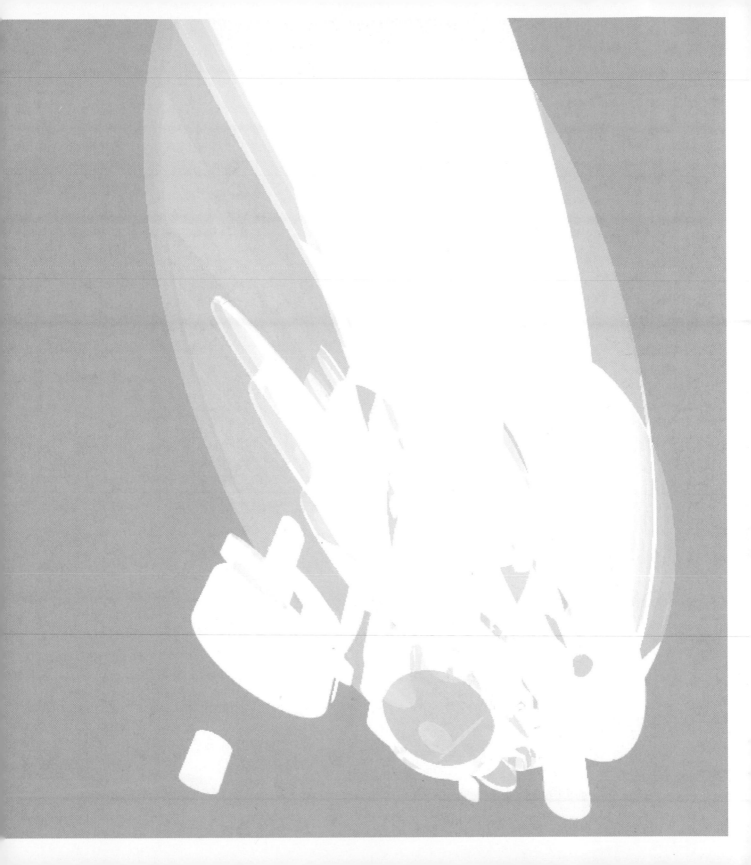

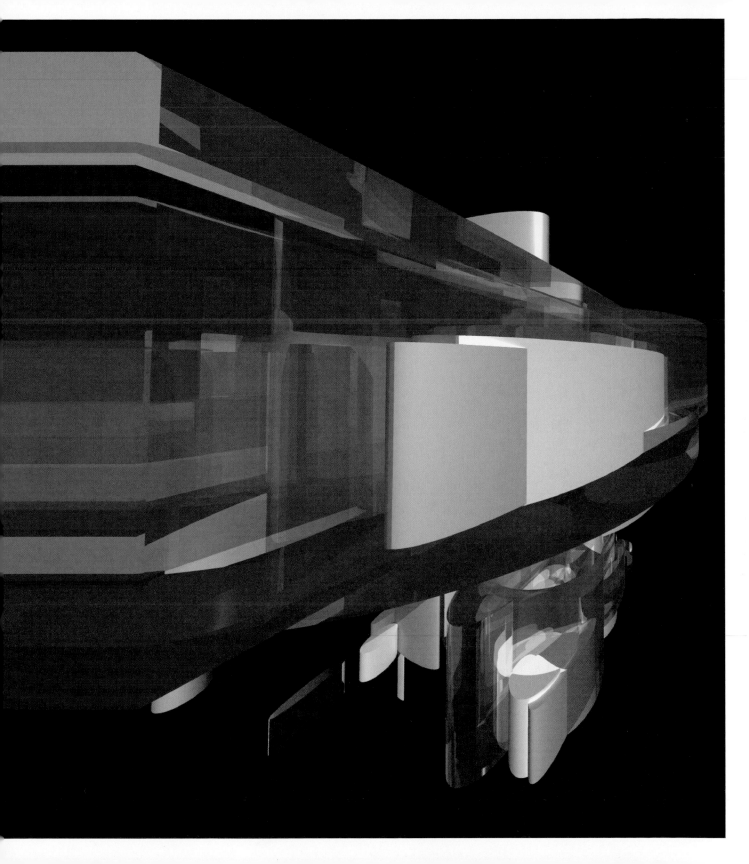

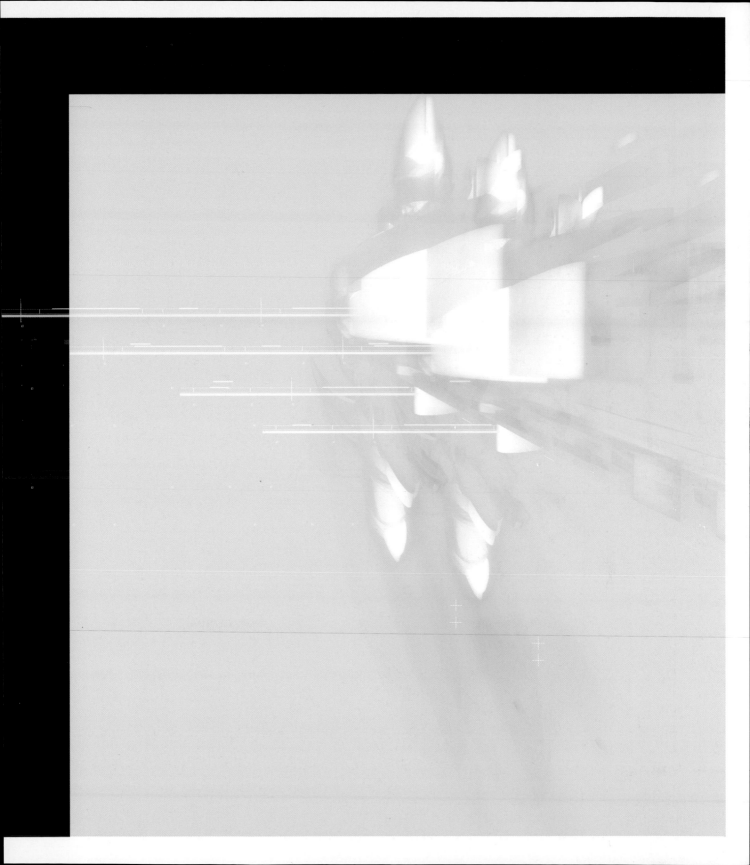

COMPLEXITY

CHAOS

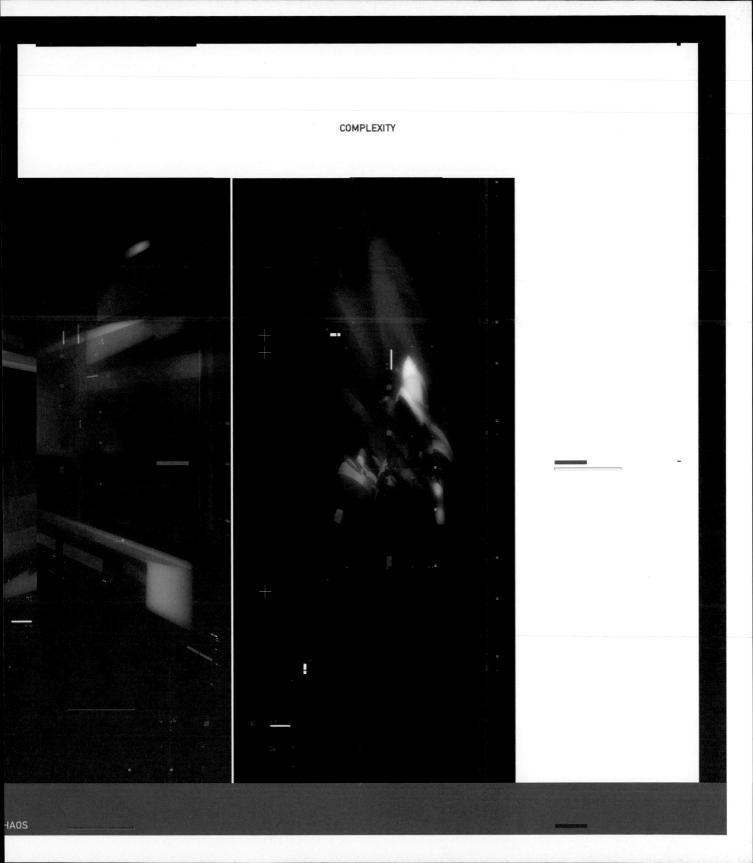

COMPLEXITY

HAOS

COMPLEXITY

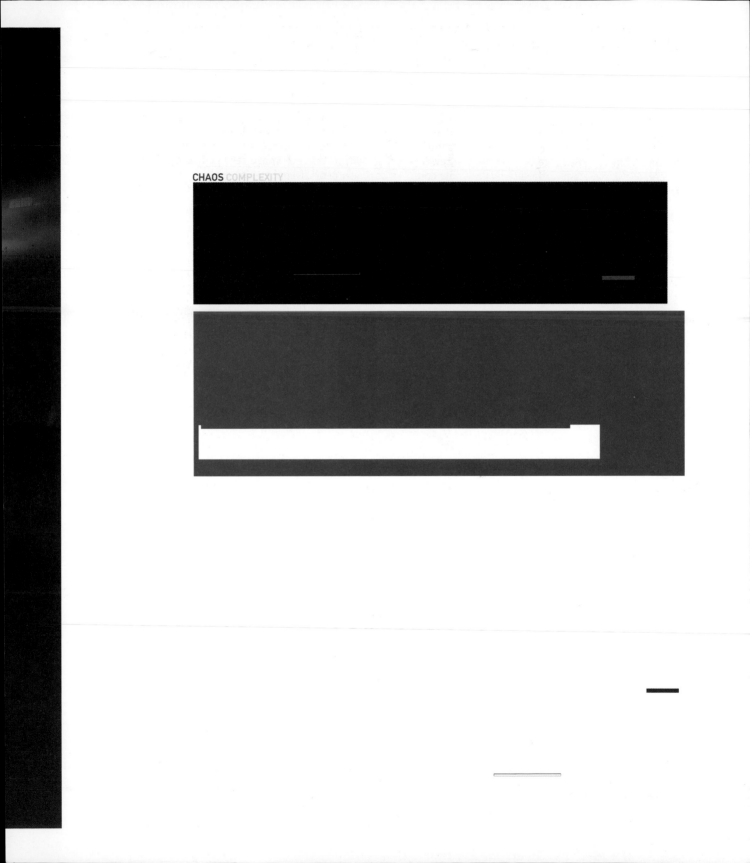

The theme that I (we) had to work with for this project was Geometry and Chaos, but I started it in the same way that I start every project: by thinking about it. This process can take anything between an hour and a day... I mostly just watch TV or read some books, starting to work out what I want to do somewhere in the back of my head. I sit down at the computer when I think of something that I like.

When I was ready to kick off the process of creation, I started up Strata 3Dpro on my Macintosh – but if you don't have it, don't worry: the cool thing about Strata is that it offers a basic version of its 3D modeling software for free download from its web site (www.strata.com).

It's not as powerful as the versions you pay for, but then I didn't use all the bells and whistles to create my model. If you want to, you can certainly use the free version to create a close facsimile for yourself, and to decide whether it suits your way of working.

What else was there to do? I created a new file, resulting in the appearance of a new window containing the default isometric perspective view. For this design, I opted for cylindrical volumes, so I simply selected the Cylinder tool from the tool bar, and started drawing cylinders randomly in the environment. As far as I was concerned, it didn't matter whether they intersected or overlapped each other (chaos, remember?).

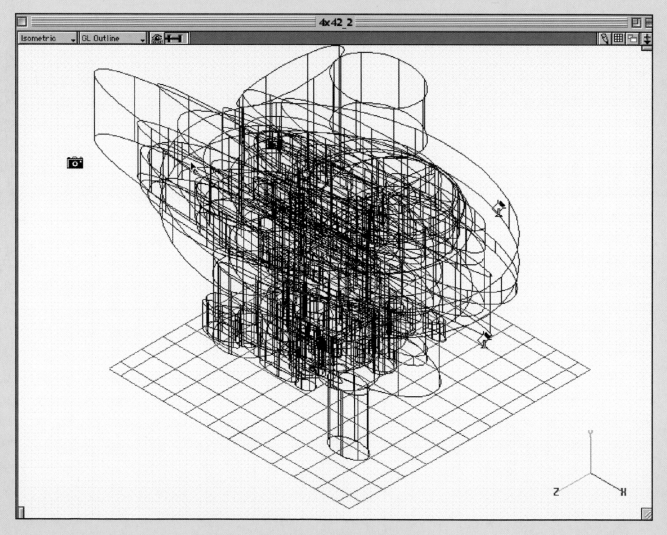

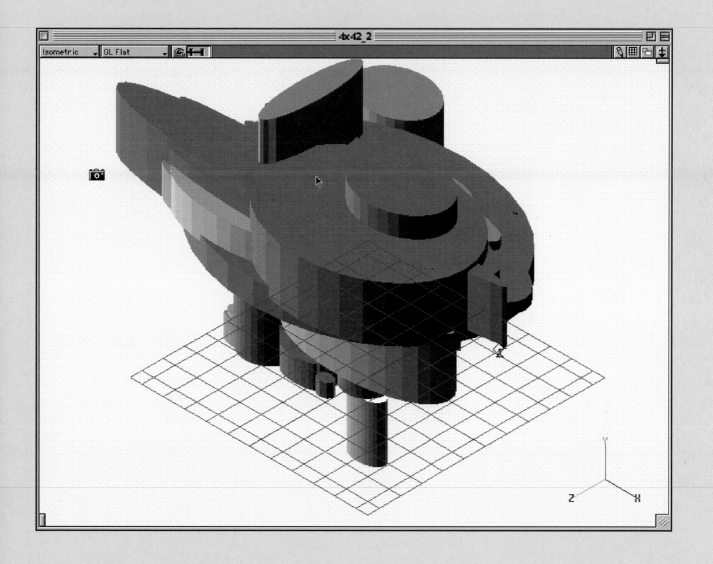

Once there were enough cylinders for my taste (in this case, around 90), I saved the file before going any further.

> Most of the time I'm working in Strata, I use the GLFlat preview mode. I find that this gives a good sense of how the whole structure looks – it's better than going with a wireframe preview, because I like to have a feel for the volume of the model I'm constructing. The GLFlat mode performs a rudimentary render of the model, so you get some sense of depth and shadow.

At this stage, I had a bunch of cylinders that all varied in size and shape, and I'll be the first to admit that it didn't look like much. My next step was to select the Camera Object tool from the tool bar, and then to set up a camera in front of the objects, but slightly off-center. Strata's camera tool is actually pretty easy to use – when you click and hold the mouse, the camera appears in that position. By dragging around, you'll see changes in the direction and angle of the lens in relation to your model, so you can position it in the way you want. If you're following along, you can now go to Windows > Camera Windows > Camera-1, and a smaller window will appear. You'll see your model through the eye of the camera, and therefore the angle from which it will be rendered.

The camera window has a slider at the top that you can move left and right in order to narrow and widen the lens respectively (you'll see the changes reflected in the main window). I tend to move my cameras quite a long way from my object(s), so that I can widen the lens to produce a pretty distorted look, which is what I'm looking for here.

I played around with the camera a little (there was no preset plan; I was just looking to convey a sense of dynamics and space), and also used the arrow buttons beneath the slider that make the camera rotate around its own x, y and z axes, and move it up, down, left, and right. Once I was happy, I closed the camera window and went back to the main work window to start sorting out the texture and color.

If the window in the screenshot below isn't already visible in the Strata interface, go to Windows > Show Resource Palette, and the preset textures will appear, grouped into categories called Textures, Shapes, FX, Gels, and Backgrounds. The Textures category is further divided into subcategories: Basic, Brick & Stone, Fun, Metal, and so on. These textures can be applied to the surfaces of the shapes in your model, mimicking the appearance of stone, wood, air, or glass (to name but a few).

Strata's software allows you to use its preset textures, to create your own textures from scratch, or to modify the preset ones in a manner of your choosing. For this image, I decided to stay with the presets – but to tweak them just a little bit, because the standard settings were too 'aggressive' for my taste. Most of the presets are very 'literal' versions of real-life textures, and they're not always as subtle as you'd want them to be.

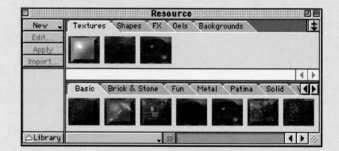

On this occasion, I chose the Glass texture by double-clicking on it, resulting in the icon being copied to the top half of the Resource palette, and the appearance of a second window. On pressing the Expert button here, you get a considerable number of options for altering the texture: you can manipulate the glossiness, light refraction, transparency, hue, color, and so on. It's actually possible to start out with Glass and change it so that it loses all of the typical characteristics of glass – but I didn't want to go that far. I just tweaked the transparency, the light refraction, and the color in order to make my objects' surfaces very transparent.

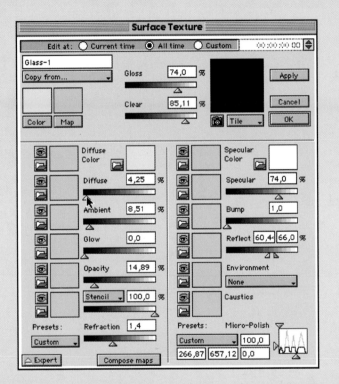

Once I'd tweaked the values, I hit the Apply button, and the modified glass texture was ready to use. To apply it to the cylinders, you just click and drag the icon over an object in the work window – when the object becomes highlighted, let go, and the texture is applied. I repeated this process until I thought that every cylinder was colored – but when I did a fast pre-render, I realized that I'd missed a few of them. I actually liked the contrast between the unaltered cylinders and the generally bluish color scheme, but the flat, plastic, 'standard' look of an uncolored object was just too dull, so I decided to give them an aluminum texture.

In the "pro" version of the Strata 3D software, the aluminum texture can be found in the Resource palette under Basic > Metal, and I went through the same steps for tweaking and applying it that I'd used for the glass. (Mainly, this involved 'softening up' the standard attributes, as I had before.) When all this was done, I closed the file and duplicated it a couple of times. Now I had multiple, identical files in which I could play around a little with lights and camera angles, without the risk of altering the original forever.

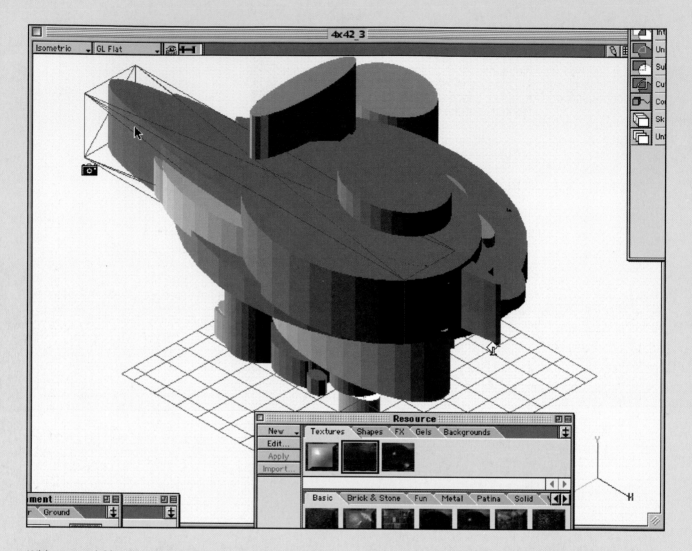

With my model in place, I started previewing the result by making some low-resolution renders. At the bottom of the floating tool bar, there's a big camera icon with a drop-down menu for specifying the rendering engine to be used; I picked Raydiosity, because I'm going to use that one for the final piece. (The Raydiosity engine, another feature of the "pro" version, is my preferred choice for objects with a lot of transparency – it gives a soft, smooth finish, while any reflections blend in nicely with the rest of the object. The Raytracing engine isn't bad, but it produces much sharper results, with more contrast. I wanted to retain the subtle light-play, and since I had the option available, I went for the former.)

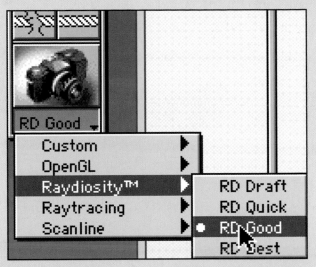

Because we're only previewing the final image at the moment, I retained the RD Good setting, which renders a scene quite quickly, with a fair amount of detail – certainly enough to get a feel for what the final outcome will look like (a wireframe or draft setting would simply represent too much of a compromise). With the Rendering Tool selected, double-clicking in any open window will cause a render of the object at the angle seen in that window. For now, it was the camera window that I was interested in.

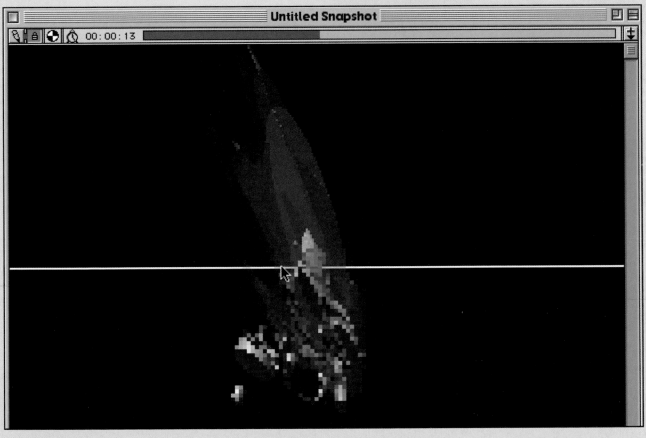

I repeated this process with all the different files I'd created so far, opening each duplicate and experimenting with camera angles and object positions, so that I could see as many different perspectives on the same scene as possible.

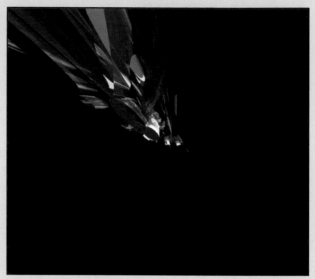

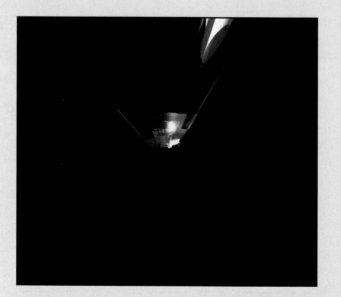

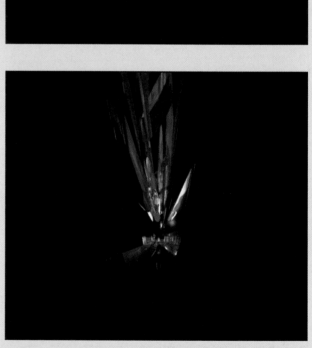

In the end, I chose views of two slightly different models for use in the final piece. They're basically the same composition, but in one of them (the first of the following images) I duplicated and superimposed some cylinders on top of the existing ones by copying, pasting, and dragging the duplicates to a position above the objects already in place. In the other file, I changed the camera angle so that I had the object cutting into the scene from the left hand side.

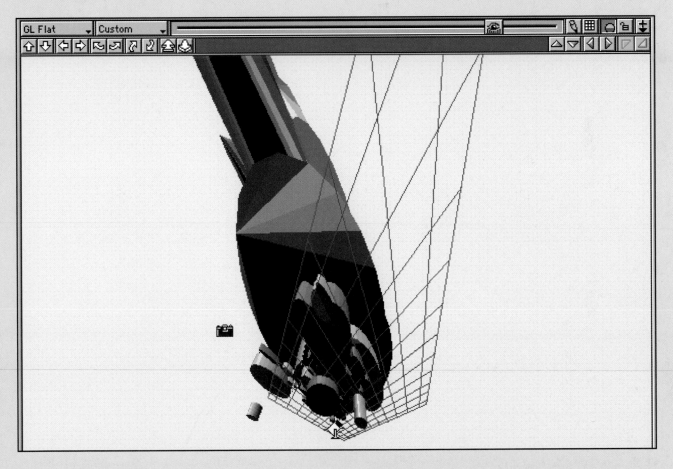

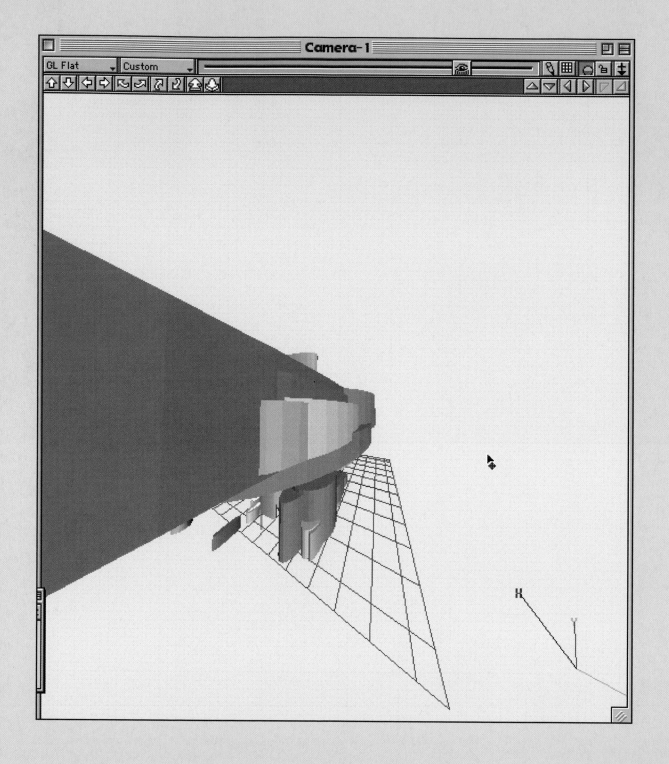

Now it was time to render for real, so I went back to the first composition, ensured that I was working in the camera window, and went to the Rendering > Render menu. The Render dialog box that appears when you do this allows you to specify the final output settings. Still using the Raydiosity rendering engine, I went for RD Best, set the Texture Detail to Fine, and the Oversampling to 9 per pixel (Extra Smooth). I made sure that the Anti-alias filter was selected, but I didn't want to render the alpha channel – opting not to do this meant that I'd end up with a completely black background.

Next, I specified the dimensions. Since my render was eventually bound for a 300dpi file, I set it to over 2000 pixels in width, with the proportions constrained so that the height scaled accordingly. I rendered the file at 72dpi (typical screen resolution), but on the result being imported into a 300dpi Photoshop document later on, I knew it would be the right size.

When all that was done, I hit the Render button, and the render began. On my machine, it took approximately an hour for each piece; obviously this will vary depending on the specifications of your computer.

"……. ……. ……. ……. ……. .   … .. ………………………………… …. "

(This is what I'm thinking about while I'm staring at my monitor, watching the render take place.)

With the renders complete, I went to File > Save As and saved them as PICT files in full color, without compression. For me, however, the raw 3D images I create are only a start. Most of the lighting effects and transparent visuals are achieved through layering my images, and by adding and erasing elements within them – and with those goals, it was time to open Photoshop and start playing!

Once in Photoshop, I created a new 300dpi document – and since it was intended for this book, I went with its page size (20.9 cm by 22.6 cm, or 2,433 pixels by 2,705 pixels). I set the background of the new file to black, opened the PICT file containing the results of my first render, selected the whole thing, and dragged it over to the empty file. The black background that Strata had rendered wasn't a problem, because I intended to work on a black background anyway – but I made the setting in Photoshop as well so that I didn't get any stray borders around the edges.

What happens next involved a lot of intuitive work – I just started playing around with the image, trying out stuff until I was happy with it. Once it was loaded, I tweaked the Levels (Image > Adjust > Levels) to add slightly more contrast, and to lighten up some of the darker areas – but not too much, because I didn't want to over-saturate it. I just wanted the darker details to be visible, and when it looked right, I applied the changes. The best advice I can give here is always to move the sliders just a little at a time, so that you'll see the subtle effects they have.

Since the glass texture I'd applied to the 3D image was bluish, some of the highlighted areas had started screaming in hellish, ultra-bright, light blue... and I certainly couldn't have that! In response, I opened the Hue/Saturation window (Image > Adjust > Hue/Saturation), and desaturated the image slightly. When I'm doing this kind of work, I tend to work directly on the image (rather than using adjustment layers) because I like to keep my files compatible with different versions of Photoshop – it's happened to me a couple of times that I've been working on an image using version 6, only to switch machines halfway through, or to send it to someone with version 5 (or even version 4) installed. Stuff can get messed up in the conversion, so I'd rather work hands-on and use duplicate layers for safety, than run the risk of not being compatible.

Once the image looked cool, I duplicated the layer, and applied an eight-pixel Gaussian blur to it. I then set the blending mode to Soft Light, and reduced the opacity to somewhere between 50 and 60%. This darkened the image a bit, giving it a soft glow. I then duplicated the original layer again, and clicked its visibility off in the Layers palette – this is my spare, in case I need it later. Because I'm not using zillions of different layers, I didn't bother to give them specific names – I tend to do that only when things start to get out of hand! Here, I was working with copies of the same layers, so I have things named layer 1 copy 2, 3, 4, and so on.

I kept repeating these actions in different parts of the composition, until I was completely satisfied with the image.

Next, I opened the PICT file containing the results of the second render, and went through the exact same process that I'd used for the first image. When I was happy with the results, I flattened the image and dragged the whole thing into my work file, on top of the rest of the layers.

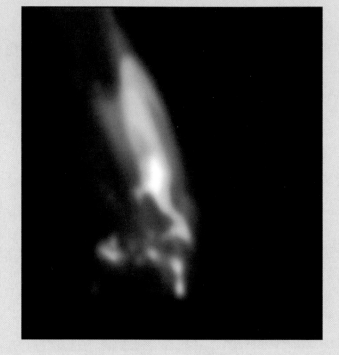

I duplicated the original layer yet again, and changed its blending mode to Multiply, reducing its opacity to 40%. The image was now very dark, and many of the subtle lights and forms were lost – but on the other hand, some parts had taken on a nice soft look, with a kind of 'underwater light' glow. In an attempt to get the best of both worlds, I selected my eraser, made two custom brushes (one of 300 pixels, and another of 500 pixels in diameter), and started erasing parts of the multiplied layer so that the covered-up parts became visible again.

Using brushes of this diameter gives you a very large but soft eraser field, so that you don't get hard edges when you erase something, but a soft edge that blends with the underlying layer. (When you use a brush with a hard edge, there's no room for subtly taking away the stuff that you don't want.)

I set the blending mode for this most recent layer to Screen, so that it became 'transparent' to the underlying layers. What this mode actually does is to 'project' the new layer on top of those beneath it – the dark areas in the top layer have little or no effect on the overall composition. I then moved the new layer around a little, and rotated it slightly so that its angle was more in sync with the rest of the image. Finally, I brushed away some small bits at the edges where it intersected with the underlying layers, preventing some of the more detailed areas from becoming too cluttered. As usual, I saved the file, duplicated it, and continued working on the duplicated file. That meant I still had my initial design, just in case something nasty happened!

By this stage, the basic design/layout was getting pretty close to what I was looking for. I flattened the file (so that the whole 3D image existed in a single layer) and repeated the whole layer-play thing again (duplicate, Gaussian blur...), tweaking it some more. The image on the right reflects the appearance of the project at the completion of this phase.

Now the 3D object itself looked nice, but it was still sitting on a flat background, and I thought that some subtle color would be an improvement. I took the Eyedropper tool and picked a blue tone from the 3D image – in this case, #465C63. Then I created a new, empty layer and filled it with this color, setting the blending mode to Soft Light, but holding the opacity at 100%. The whole image received the same overall blue tone, which darkened it slightly, but that was all right; I liked it that way.

I was less happy, though, with the way the flat color took away some of the depth of the image, so I created another layer with the aim of doing something about it. In the tool bar, I set the background color to black (the foreground color was still the blue tone), selected the Gradient tool, and drew a gradient in the empty layer from the bottom straight upwards, so that the darkest part was at the bottom of the image. I set the blending mode to Screen, resulting in the image gaining some depth, but making the whole piece very light, losing some subtle detail. In response, I lowered the opacity of the new layer to 30-40%, so that the image regained some of its contrast. To finish it off, I applied some noise to the layer (Filter > Noise > Add Noise...) so the gradient became a little softer still.

To my mind, the 3D composition was now complete, but I felt that the dynamics weren't working; I didn't like the angle at which the object was 'cutting into' the page. I started rotating the image clockwise in 90° steps, until I ended up back at the initial view. As a result of this process, I decided that the image was much more pleasing upside down, so I rotated the canvas through 180° and left it there. Now the composition cut in from the top-middle/top right – I'd achieved a much more 'in your face' effect that brought out the dynamic of the 3D image.

Feeling the need to add still more substance and detail to the image, I went back to my first, unflattened, work file, selected the layer with the first 3D object, and dragged it over to the working file, positioning it between the Soft Light blue-colored layer and the Gradient layer. After all my modifications, the colors of the original were slightly out of sync with those in the rest of the image, adding some depth to it. I rotated this layer (Edit >Transform > Rotate 180°) so that it fitted with the rest of the composition.

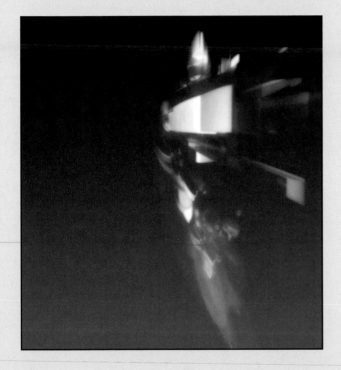

At this stage, the major features of the image were at last complete, and it was time to add some details and distortions. I never intended the image to be 'just' a 3D composition – I wanted to add more to it, by including some fine detail that would produce a more technical appearance. These details and distortions would also add to the theme of Geometry and Chaos, and would include grids placed over the image to give a sense of structure. For these aspects, I found inspiration from technical diagrams, elements of pie charts, architectural plans... nothing in particular, but any little elements that held my attention and got stuck in my head.

By now, I'd saved the Photoshop file, duplicated it again, and started working on the duplicate. Before going any further, I also flattened the image once more: I was happy with the basic design and wanted to get the file size down – my computer was starting to complain!

I created all the tiny details at 72dpi, so that they would become very small and subtle on being imported into the main 300dpi file. An additional benefit is that you can work on a 72dpi file at 100% magnification, and therefore retain a good overview of the whole thing. Furthermore, it helps to keeps the file size down, because lots of extra detail can really add to the layer count. Once I'd designed the details, I merged (as opposed to flattened) all the layers, so that they remained separate from the background, and dragged the merged layer to my work file. As usual, I duplicated this new layer a couple of times, because I was planning on using it more than once.

My next move was to distort/add perspective to the new layer (Edit > Transform > Distort or Perspective), so that it married properly with the existing imagery. That done, I set the blending mode to Soft Light, creating the effect that the details were 'embedded' in the 3D object. I then duplicated the layer I'd just operated on, set the blending mode to Normal, and erased some parts of it. The result of this was that some of details became highlighted, adding yet more depth to that area of the image, and further enhancing the feeling that the details actually were part of the 3D composition, rather than simply having been laid on top of it.

I did this again on another part of the 3D image, so that the details weren't concentrated in one place. After that, I shuffled my 'extra' detail layers around, until I found a place where they complemented the overall image. Then, I continued to add more little features (like subtle crosshairs) until I was completely satisfied.

Finally, to add some more abstract elements to the composition, I went right back to the bottom layer containing the 3D image, selected a piece of the image that was only one pixel wide, and copied and pasted it into a new layer. Then I started copying the layer, offsetting it a pixel at a time to create a field. (This takes easily 100 layers, but these are merged immediately.) I then rotated that layer 45° clockwise, cutting away until I got the forms I was looking for, and placed them over the main image. This was a tricky process, but doing things this way gave me total control over the nature and effect of the offsetting.

At last, the whole image was finished. I flattened it, and doubled the canvas size so that the format became a double-page spread. Then I started to play with the layout, adding color fields and some additional details and text. No fancy tricks or shortcuts were used here; I just used basic rectangular shapes and the like to fill out the design. You can see the result – my completed piece – on the following pages. For now, thank you for listening... and good luck in your future work.

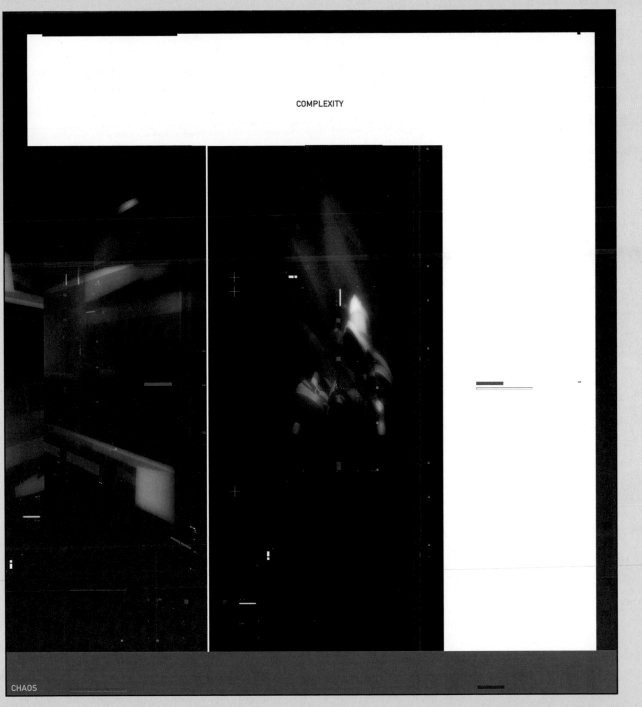

COMPLEXITY

CHAOS

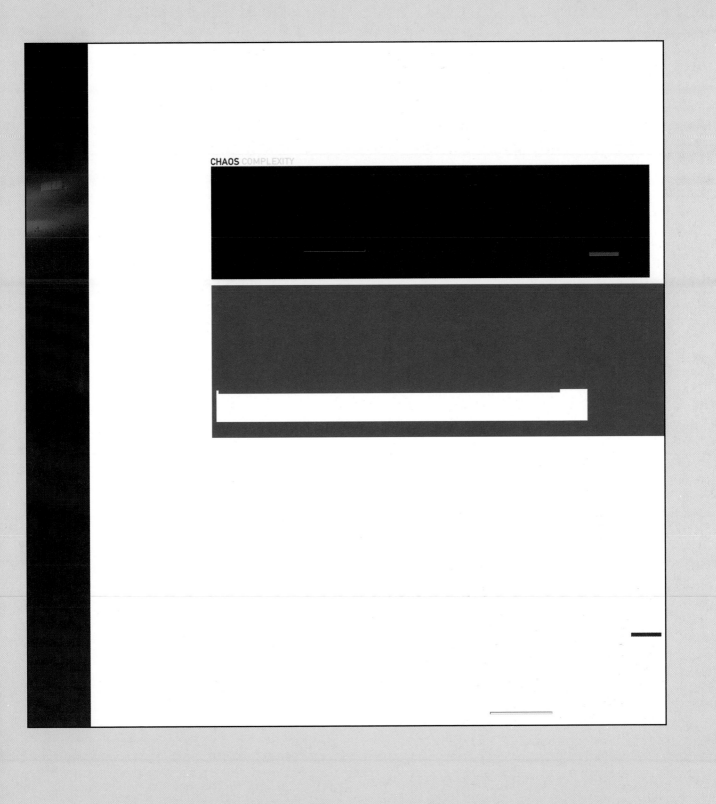

CHAOS COMPLEXITY

Each author was invited to remix the other works submitted for the book, and the following pages display the resulting hybrid pieces. *Noise* is the sound of the private discussion forum in which the authors answered questions and discussed the project with each other. *Interference* details each author's responses to the challenge of remixing.

ED: What was your initial response to the other 3 artists' work? (Were you surprised? Disappointed? Intrigued? Impressed?)

Brian: I would have to say that I was impressed. I could only go by the limited work I'd seen by the other artists online, but I could tell that they were all very good at what they do, and I knew they all would come up with something interesting. I wasn't disappointed.

 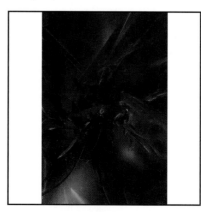 

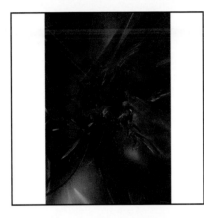

Dave: My first reaction was a simple, "Damn! That's good 3D." All the pieces definitely carried the theme of *Geometry and Chaos*, but they all had their own voices, because the approaches were all different. This kind of variety was something that I had hoped for, and I wasn't disappointed.

I'd assumed certain things about the style with which each artist was going to approach the subject, and to a certain extent I was on the mark, but only in the loosest sense. I knew that Brian was an awesome modeler, and that his textures would be great, but I had no idea of the lengths he would go to in the pursuit of that. I knew Nathan's work would be visually rich, but I was still knocked over by the colors. Tom's was easier to get a hold of, because his approach looked like it was going down the same mathematical route that I'd taken – but the images themselves were stunning, and represented a part of something that I hadn't considered.

To me, the individual pieces reflect parts of what we had each tried before in other work, but they all have something new about them. Having all four images open on my desktop at once gave me a very good feeling about how this book was going to shape up. I hope that everyone else felt the same!

Nathan: The first piece I saw was Dave's, and the first thing I thought was, "Whoa! I would never have thought of going that direction." His simplistic approach, with the invasion of chaos and mathematics, was executed extremely well.

Shortly after, I saw Tom's, and again I was impressed. Very nicely done, and a two-page layout, too.

Finally, I got to see what Brian was working on, and I had no idea how much he had done. I was pretty shocked – for a moment, I felt like I hadn't done enough.

The best thing, though, was to see how everyone's work was completely different, and yet it all was built with the same objective. Like Brian, after I saw everything together, I knew this book was going to be special.

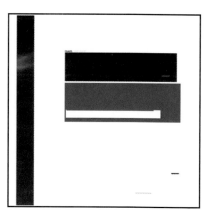

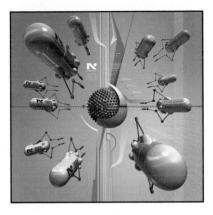

Tom: I was very impressed when I saw the other work, too – it gives a nice variety to the whole concept of the book. It was really interesting to see how the different styles and ideas gave form to the same brief... you can definitely tell that all the images are linked to the same theme.

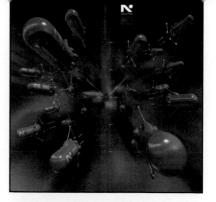

ED: Has your opinion changed over time, at all? Considering each work in turn, what are your favorite and least favorite aspects? Given the chance, what would you alter?

Brian: My opinion hasn't changed over time – and to answer the last part of the question, I don't really feel that it's up to me to suggest changes to something that someone else has produced. I feel that the success of pieces of work like these is largely down to the viewer's own interpretation of what they see in them. For that reason, I don't think it's necessarily a good idea for an artist to explain exactly what a piece of work means – part of that should be left to the viewer.

Nathan's piece works particularly well in that respect – it's so beautifully complex that I'm sure everyone must see something different in it, and that's definitely a good thing. Personally, I see nature in there, with forms reminiscent of plants and insects, but someone else may have quite another perception.

When you look into it, Tom's piece has a lot of detail going on too, and there's a nice photographic quality to it. I keep seeing high-tech television monitors in there – but again, regardless of what was intended, it looks good and that's what matters.

Dave's piece works by virtue of its simplicity, and I think it was a brave move to produce something that doesn't obviously look 3D. The 'flat' 3D style is becoming popular at the moment, and this is a good example of the technique.

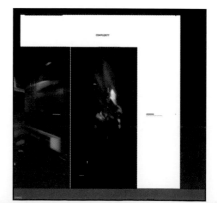

Dave: Like Brian, I'm as satisfied with the all the works now as I was when I first viewed them. If I had to be specific, I'm still stunned hy the colors and the layouts.

As for altering things, I prefer to talk about collaboration, because I don't know that it's my responsibility to mess with someone else's work. It wasn't necessary for me to be there during the initial build, so why should I be there at the end, inflicting my own ideas on what somebody else considers to be a completed work? I think that the remixes I've done will represent some of my own philosophies, while maintaining the integrity of the original designs.

Nathan: The same goes for me. Everything is just as impressive as the first time I saw it. As for altering anyone else's pieces, I don't feel I have any reason to do so. Had this project not required us to do remixes, I would never have thought about altering anyone else's work.

Tom: My opinion hasn't changed since the first time I saw the artwork either. Like Brian, I only knew the caliber and styles of the other designers from the work they post on their sites, but when you look at the pieces everyone did, no one tried to reinvent themselves. Everyone stayed true to their vision and style, and that gives a really tight look overall.

ED: Do you think the other artists have responded well to the theme they were presented with? What about their work makes you say that?

Brian: It's difficult to say for sure without reading their essays and finding out about the reasons behind the work they've produced. The theme is so broad that it's potentially open to just about anything. Coupled with the fact that the designers all work in an abstract style, a very wide range of interpretations is possible.

Nathan: I definitely think that they have responded well. It's amazing how you can take one objective and go in so many different directions with it.

I'm fairly familiar with each of the other authors' work, but I can't say that I've ever seen Brian do anything involving any sort of chaos, so it was great to see his work go in that direction.

Tom: It's a tough question, because I don't feel like I'm in a position to criticize my peers. We all clearly have different styles, and to say something about the other works would therefore only be grounded in personal preference. All I can say is that if you look at it objectively, all the works here represent the given theme. But they all do it in their own way, and you can't say that one is 'right' and another 'wrong'.

Dave: Again, the things that impressed me most were the variety of interpretations and methods of execution. The subject matter lent itself well to a wide range of renditions; I think the diversity in the work speaks to that, and represents a good cross-section of the possible ways of approaching the theme.

ED: On the flip side, how do you feel about your own work when set against the others?

Brian: The first thing I would have to say is that I maybe went a little over the top compared with the other artists, but I'm quite happy with the way my work turned out, and I feel that it sits quite nicely alongside the other works.

Nathan: I don't really feel any reason to compare my work with the others' work. I do feel, however, that everyone's work together makes a great mix for this project.

Dave: I see tweaks here and there that I'd like to make to my piece now, but it's a pretty good representation of what I've done in the past, and of some methodologies I may continue to use in the future. I wish I'd thought to do a two-pager like Tom did, though.

Tom: I feel happy, because in my opinion they're all super-talented, and at the top of what they do. When you stand next to something that looks great, some of that rubs off on you. I don't think you can say that one is better than another; it's like trying to compare apples and oranges. They each have their own value, but they're all very different.

ED: Regarding the technical aspects of the other works, what can you learn from? Is there anything in your contribution that you'd now approach differently?

Brian: I wouldn't say that I've learned much from a technical point of view, but I'm sure I've taken something from the works aesthetically and stored them in the back of my mind for possible rip-off purposes at a later date. (Only joking!) But no, I don't think I would have done anything different for my contribution had I seen the others' work beforehand.

Nathan: I think it's sort of difficult to answer this question, because I don't see things at a technical level. I'm not big on 'tricks' or anything else, I just like to create forms and build from them. I don't see the other artists' work as, "OK, he used a blur here, he used the lasso tool over here, and he cut that there." That doesn't interest me at all. It's all about the end product.

Dave: I honestly don't do tutorials, so I'm not sure I can say much here. Even after reading the other guys' work, I was more in tune with their impressions than with the technical aspects. I like to hear about other people's ways of operating before they actually sit down to make something. That's one of the reasons why I felt the need to document so many of my impressions in my tutorial. Technically, there were a few "so that's how they did that" moments, but I haven't rushed out to duplicate their processes.

Tom: The person whose tutorial I felt closest to was Brian, especially the 3D part – he's an Infini-D power user, and I use that program a lot too. The depth-of-field technique is actually quite obvious, but it seems that Brian is one of the only guys to use it to create realistic pieces. Nathan and Dave both used 3ds max, and since I'm 100% Mac-based, I didn't really bother to go into the details.

Dave: To me, this book was more effective as a journey of processes, than as a technical study. I really liked hearing about the guys' approaches, rather than how they bumped a pixel here and there. Theory over execution has always been my approach to science in general. I hate litmus paper.

Brian: They're certainly a good example of one of the directions 3D is headed today, but I don't think four people could possibly represent all the techniques present in 3D work. I personally like all kinds of other 3D styles that don't happen to be present in this book. Some of my current favorite exponents of 3D would include:

Me Company (www.mecompany.com), Futurefarmers (www.futurefarmers.com), Shynola (www.shynola.freeserve.co.uk), and Attik (www.attik.com).

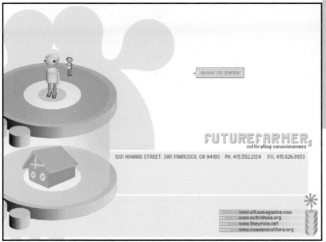

© www.futurefarmers.com 2001

ED: Looking at the styles of the four artists here, do you think they form a good snapshot of where 3D design is headed today? Are any contemporary techniques obviously missing? Who are the best exponents of those styles?

Dave: I don't know; I think this book contains a pretty good representation of what's out there. From the more technically proficient to more rudimentary usage, I think the four pieces cover a wide range of 3D design and methods of traditional layout.

There are some obvious gaps, though, when you consider some of the traditional uses for 3D programs – specifically, gaming and motion picture usage. Professional modelers and special effects gurus in the entertainment industry could fill those gaps that we designers may not have had the expertise to fill.

Nathan: I think that what the other artists have done is a great example of where 3D is heading today. It's particularly great to see that there's more to 3D than simply modeling what already exists. Abstract forms are my favorites, and I see more and more things going abstract.

It's important to know about contemporary and traditional techniques for every medium, but I don't really stress on making myself follow those techniques. I don't really like following the 'rules'.

Tom: Hmm... when you look at the pieces, you get a nice overview of different modeling styles: Brian is very product- and object-oriented, Dave is very focused on mathematical models, while Nathan and I go completely abstract – we just start modeling until we come up with nice forms and compositions, and work from there. I think that if you look around in the design community, those are the main styles. I can't pinpoint one or more exponents, though, because each style can be broken down into a million different sub-styles and hybrids.

ED: All of the works in the book have an abstract element to them. Brian does less abstract stuff in Rustboy; do the rest of you feel that abstract is where you'll always be happiest – or do you sometimes have a terrible urge to go out and do a big image of a marble ball on a chessboard?

Nathan: I'm definitely happiest doing abstract. Normal = boring.

Dave: I spend a good 70% of my time doing client work day in and day out, and that kind of literal communication tends to get pretty painful after a while. Some of my more abstract designs have been direct rebuttals to periods of extremely stressful work. As long as I'm cranking out sites with crappy logos, and continuing to deal with less-than-malleable clients, I imagine I'll be generating this kind of work. It's a classic Catch-22 that Yossarian himself would be surprised by.

ED: What collaborative projects have you tried in the past? Do you think this one has worked? Does collaboration usually result in a lack of focus, or is the sum greater than its parts? Is it a traumatic or emphatic process?

Dave: Outside of the day-to-day grind of a job, where collaboration is pretty much essential, I usually just let loose on my own. And to be honest, I haven't had much opportunity for collaboration with other artists in the past. The opportunity to do some cooperative work for this project was pretty exciting, and one of its more attractive features for me. My only reservation was that the integrity of everyone's pieces should remain, despite any remixes that I may effect. It's pretty nerve-wracking to subject someone else's work to your personal processes. It was even a little schizophrenic at times.

Brian: I haven't really done very much in the way of collaboration in the past. Probably the most collaborative piece I've worked on has been *dodge* magazine, which involved thirteen people with very different styles. They were forced to work within a limited color palette in order to give the online magazine a cohesive look.

I think collaboration can be a disaster if people are given too much of a free rein, and it generally works better if there's a tight format, theme, or set of restrictions from the outset to help bind the work together.

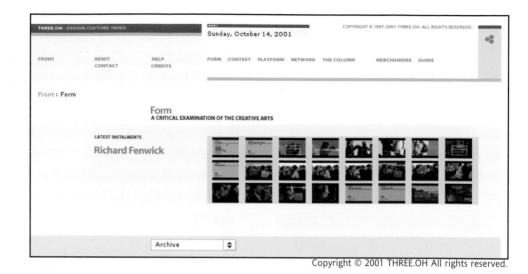

Nathan: I've actually done quite a few collaborative works with other people, and it's always been great fun. It can be quite an exercise, because mixing two styles together isn't always an easy thing to do – but challenges are good!

The entire second version of NGINCO (Surveillance) was a collaborative project between me and my friend Herman Leung, who is the other half of NGINCO. It was a great experience: our styles are similar but definitely different, and it was great to see how everything worked together.

I've also worked on several projects with James Widegren, who is the creative officer of THREE.OH. Those projects were not only exciting; they also pushed us both to new levels.

Working with someone else, or as part of a team, always allows for more forward motion and more breaking of rules, and I think it's great.

Tom: When I take part in collaborations, I'm usually in a position to handpick my collaborators for myself. And most of the time you do collaborations, it's just for fun: a style exercise.

For example, the last collaboration I did was a series of stock images for Digital Vision with Stoav, whom I've known since high school, and we had a blast. We know each other's styles, and feel we can fill out each other's work. I think the most important aspect of collaborations is mutual respect for each other's style and opinion. With this book, we really didn't know what the other guy was going to do, so there was a constant level of excitement and curiosity.

ED: Why do you do this stuff, and who do you think your audience is? Do you think that design for design's sake will become a more mainstream art form?

Nathan: I do what I do because I enjoy what I do, and I suppose that my audience consists of people who enjoy what I do.

I definitely believe that design for design's sake will become more of an art form. As I said in my essay, I don't consider what I do to *be* design – to me, it's digital art.

Dave: I do it because it's fun! If I didn't enjoy doing it, I'd probably have moved onto something else by now. As to my audience, I've never been quite sure of that. Who likes useless 3D objects, anyhow?

I tend to think of art and design as aspects of communication, so I don't know if it will ever be 'just' design to me. Communication design has spanned the ages, from the doodles just to the left of ancient cave paintings, to the works of David Carson. I don't know that this project is anything but a continuation of that process.

Brian: Presumably, "this stuff" means experimental, personal work? I think the main reason people do it is because they can. It's a contrast to the commercial work people generally have to do in their daily life, and the beauty is that you have no one to answer to.

When you talk about an online portfolio, your audience is potentially huge. There has never been a way of getting your work across to so many people, at a cost of virtually nothing.

I think experimental work does gradually filter into the mainstream – at least, it always has done in the past. Think of something like MTV: I'm not necessarily saying that it's good design, but it certainly uses graphic styles that would once have been regarded as weird and experimental, but are now taken for granted by the general public.

Tom: I do it for the love of the game. I've always been creative in one way or another, and I've reached a point where my work is my hobby, and vice versa. I like creating things, and learning while doing so – enriching myself with new ideas and techniques.

It would be nice to see design for design's sake becoming a mainstream art form, but we mustn't forget that (graphic) design is first and foremost a way of communication – it's *more* than art for art's sake. That said, there have been countless examples where design (be it graphic, furniture, or even product design) has been elevated to art over time... so I guess it all depends on general acceptance, and the period in history.

ED: Has your work changed radically over time? Have there been any significant shocks to your system that have changed your working methods?

Brian: Yes – in fact, I'd say that my work changes radically *all* the time. I'm never happy sticking with one style. Even when I worked in traditional illustration for years, I wasn't the kind of illustrator who was known for one particular style; I preferred to work in a variety of completely different styles. Without a doubt, the most significant shock to my system has been the computer, which opened up avenues unavailable through traditional methods.

Dave: I hope that my work shows an evolution, and that the process is still continuing. I've been exposed to some great people (not just digital artists) who have helped me immensely. They've provided inspiration when I've needed it, and a kick in the ass when I needed that more.

        I think that a good kick in the ass qualifies as a shock to the system!

Nathan: My work has definitely changed over time, and I go through different phases. Sometimes I'm in a more 'minimal' mode, where I simply want to work with form, and not create too much depth. Other times, I want to create something so detailed that you really have to look deep into the piece to see it. Most recently, I've been playing a bit with some photography, and creating some extremely 'messy' pieces.

Tom: 'Radical' would be an understatement! When in college, I was a layer maniac – the more complex I could make an image, the better. Later on, when working for a lot of corporate clients, I had to restrain myself in order to make sites that were easy accessible, and that changed my way of thinking a lot in terms of composition, design, and usability. Nowadays I'm much more interested and focused on the relationships between different aspects of design – and the 'less is more' principle.

ED: At a higher level, is there any medium that doesn't work for you, or doesn't contain the tensions required for artistic expression? Conversely, is there a medium you've yet to explore, but which seems to hold a lot of promise?

Brian: I'm quite sure there are media I've yet to explore, but I can't think of any particular examples right now. I still feel like I've just scratched the surface of the possibilities offered by the computer, and there are sure to be many avenues to explore there alone.

I'm just starting to experiment with DVD technology, which I find very exciting, but I'm not sure if you would class that as a medium as such.

Nathan: There are a few media, particularly motion and print, that I've really been ready to head into lately. I would like to get deeper into 3D as well. One thing I'd like to do someday is to create a music video.

Dave: I'm still trying to master this online/interactive thing! It's still got loads of potential, once the yahoos who design browsers can get together to create some universal standards.

Tom: I think that all avenues of design are interesting to explore. For me, the most fascinating thing is that each discipline you work in has its own boundaries – and therein lays the challenge. The things you can do in print or motion can't be accomplished on the Web – or maybe they can, but in a different way. That search to find new ways of bypassing boundaries, or using them to your advantage, is what makes it exciting. It doesn't matter much to me what discipline I'm active in, as long it's creative, and there's room to grow artistically and personally.

ED: Do you have a definite idea about what direction you're headed in the future?

Brian: Not really. I never plan anything like that; I prefer to let fate take me in new directions. I've always known that I would work in the art/design field, but I've never really set out to do anything in particular – I just seem to fall into new areas somehow. It's worked so far, so I may as well continue wandering aimlessly through the world of design and see what crops up.

Nathan: 3D, and motion, and print. The Web is extremely tired right now.

Dave: I'm heading east, and I might veer north for a while if the snow's good, but ultimately I'll probably just end up where I started before I went eastward.

Tom: If I can stay on track with the things I'm doing now, I'll be a very happy man. I don't have any plans set in concrete – the only things I know I'd like to do are to write some books on interior design vs. graphic design. Being a college professor is something that's in the back of my head too – I think it would be a nice thing to ready the next wave of designers. Oh, and maybe doing some comics would be cool too.

Dave: I'd like to be more print-based eventually, and to have more to do with information architecture rather than straight-up pixel jockeying. Deciding how an aesthetic best translates into ideas and philosophies is still fairly exciting to me – it's just seldom implemented these days. I don't think the Web's that stagnant, but I'd like to see some more thoughtful designs being generated.

ED: Nathan makes an interesting point about the tiredness of the Web. Is that something that strikes a chord with the rest of you? Do motion and print work hold the same appeal for you as they do for him?

Brian: I don't work in web design (XL5 and Rustboy are my first-ever attempts). I come from a print background already, but I'd definitely like to get into motion design.

Nathan: I think that what it all comes down to is this: You will hardly ever get a web client that lets you have fun. There are rare occasions, true, but it's still 'design', and I don't like that.

And on top of that, the Web is a childish thing. The way that some people act is just ridiculous, and nothing like that (that I'm aware of) has been seen in print or motion.

I don't know; I'm just tired of it. Working on my own site is fine, but I plan on doing that less and less as well.

Dave: As I see it, part of my job is to educate even as I'm providing other services, so as a project proceeds through different phases of production, stuff will (hopefully) work itself out. That said, I find that clients generally can be fairly tough to deal with, due to the flexible nature of the Web. Explaining screen resolutions, default browser settings, and basic requirements for deployment on the Web becomes pretty tiresome at times.

Dave: Learning new stuff makes working with computers worthwhile – otherwise it's just sacrificing days, weeks, and years for a crappy tan and a potbelly.

Tom: Basically, I don't care that much if I'm doing web, print, or motion design. As long as I can be creative and learn stuff along the way, I'll be a happy man.

ED: But when you're working for corporations all the time, can't creativity be very restricted?

Brian: Yes, corporate work can be boring as hell, but thankfully I'm not really doing that kind of thing these days. Up until recently, I worked for about a year in a computer games company (not as exciting as it sounds), and for the past few months my full-time job has been doing 3D concept work for a TV production company. It's kind of a weird one – I was lucky enough to call the shots, so I work from home in my own time, but I get paid a full salary. So I'm pretty much getting to where I want to be these days.

Tom: I don't think the Web is saturated at all. Sure, it's in a slump right now, but there are still so many untapped opportunities.

One example of that is the site I just did for Ashley Wood (www.ashleywood.com) – I got a load of mail from the comic book community saying that they'd never seen a site like that. (Flash animation, sound, very design-oriented...)

To me, this is proof that we can only see the tip of the iceberg. There are probably millions of companies, in all kinds of industries, who are still unaware of 'design' sites.

On the other hand, I'm also getting back to doing some more print-based stuff, because that's where I came from. It's always nice to be able to hold your work in your hands.

Brian: The Ashley Wood site is excellent, Tom, and a brilliant example of what's possible. Your style, combined with the content, works so well – and I can see how it would appeal to a wide range of people.

WWW.ASHLEYWOOD.COM
MAIN NODE
WELCOME TO ASHLEY WOOD

TITLE
ASHLEYWOOD

ABOUT NEWS GALLERY STORE RELATED
DOWNLOAD CONTACT CREDITS

ASHLEYWOOD

Tom: Thanks, Brian! I just got lucky that Ashley was very open to my suggestions and style. Stuff like that doesn't always happen overnight.

Nathan: I agree that the Web isn't tired; I'm just personally tired of it. There are so many things that haven't been done, and so many things that can be refined, and so many new rules to make and break. Right now it just doesn't interest me.

And I agree: the site you did for Ashley Wood was excellent, Tom.

ED: Looking to the future, if you had the expertise and money to create the ultimate image manipulation/digital design software, what would it do? What constrains you in current applications?

Brian: Personally, I'm quite happy with Photoshop. I think that in most cases, constraints aren't down to the software, but the people who use it. Photoshop is so open-ended that I'm sure it's capable of just about anything, as long as someone with the imagination to make it happen is using it.

I don't like the direction some software is going – trying to make it easy for the user by doing everything for you. This is killing creativity, and it's the reason why so many people's work looks the same these days. You should have to think about how you're going to achieve something, and figure out ways of getting round problems. That way, it's far less likely that people will come up with the same solution, and the result would surely be more diverse work.

Nathan: That would take a long time to think about, but the one thing I'd wish to see in the *near* future is a z-axis in Photoshop. That would change... everything.

Dave: If I had that much expertise, and that much money, I'd retire!

The only constraint that bugs me is rendering, and the time involved. In the past I've sometimes found it hard to explain to my boss that the little blue line marching across the screen is actually me working.

Tom: Whoo, that's a tough one! First of all, I think I'd develop a standard browser that runs smoothly on every platform possible. (OK, that's not *actually* an image manipulation tool, but I think it's something of importance to me and my fellow web designers.)

As for image manipulation tools... I don't really know... I don't think I'd try to come up with one magic application. Instead, I'd focus on compatibility between existing ones, to smoothen the workflow when you're multitasking with different applications.

ED: And finally... who would have been your three dream collaborators, living or dead? Why?

© Kyle Cooper and Jenny Shainin, *Imaginary Forces*

© Kyle Cooper and Jenny Shainin, *Imaginary Forces*

Brian: This is so difficult to do, but I eventually went for three diverse people/companies who have consistently impressed me. They're not necessarily best known for working with still images, but here are my choices:

[1] Moebius.
[2] Chris Cunningham.
[3] Imaginary Forces.

Moebius (Jean Giraud) is a French comic book artist who was a big inspiration to me when I was younger. He also inspired Ridley Scott (another hero of mine), and his influence can clearly be seen in both Alien and Blade Runner.

The first time I encountered Chris Cunningham's work was on the *Come To Daddy* video for Aphex Twin. That video just blew me away at the time, and I've been impressed with everything else he's done since. Genius.

Imaginary Forces are best known for producing movie title sequences. The titles for *Seven* first grabbed my attention, and they've produced many other excellent sequences since.

Dave: Jim Henson, because I've dreamed of working in his creature shop ever since I was old enough to realize Oscar was just a little guy with his hand up a puppet's ratty green butt.

George Lucas, circa 1980. Back then, he was the original Jedi Knight, and in the prime of his career.

Kyle Cooper and Imaginary Forces. I'll sometimes sit down when I'm bored and watch the credits to *Seven*, just to get my mind blown. I like them spooky pictures!

Nathan: This is kind of tough.

The work of Lebbeus Woods, the American architect, is absolutely amazing. He creates abstract architecture in the most chaotic manner I have ever seen. Hooking up with him would be fascinating.

Once I get more into motion, it would be amazing to work with Chris Cunningham some day. There's nothing else to say other than that he is incredible, and has created some of the most amazing pieces I've ever seen (*All Is Full Of Love*, and *Come To Daddy*, for example).

Kyle Cooper, creator of the *Seven* credits, would also be incredible to work with. Those credits are by far the best I have ever seen, and since I've been doing some 'messy' work recently, they have interested me even more. I could watch them forever, I think.

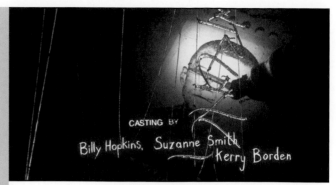

© Kyle Cooper and Jenny Shainin, *Imaginary Forces*

Tom: If I had to pick three dream collaborators today, I would go with:

a) mOrphosis (www.morphosis.net) – an American architecture agency that's realized some of the most cutting-edge and refreshing architectural design over the years. It's actually more of a conceptual think tank than an agency, always testing the boundaries of its field. If mOrphosis were unavailable, Zaha Hadid would be very high on my wish list too, for the same reasons.

b) Mike Mignola – the comic book artist, well known for his occult comic book series Hellboy. In my opinion, Mignola is a master of minimalist art, and the way he draws and designs his pages is always perfect.

c) Warren Ellis – an English writer, active in the comic book world, and best known for his work on The Authority and Planetary. His stories and concepts are larger than life – it would be interesting to design or illustrate the things he comes up with.

Brian: Well, isn't that interesting? Out of the four of us, two have chosen Chris Cunningham, and three chose Kyle Cooper/Imaginary Forces.

Nathan: I was actually at Imaginary Forces the other day, but I didn't see Kyle Cooper there – or at least, I wasn't introduced to him.

It's really cool, though, that Kyle Cooper and Chris Cunningham showed up in our responses. Proves we're on the same wavelength, or something...

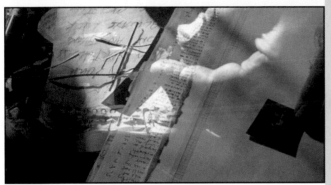

© Kyle Cooper and Jenny Shainin, *Imaginary Forces*

Tom: In my answers, I didn't really want to limit myself to the design world – although I would love to work with Imaginary Forces. When Seven came out, I was well underway in college – and seeing that sequence, coupled with discovering Carson and *Emigre* magazine, made me realize that there was this whole untapped world of possibilities for expressing yourself graphically.

On the other hand, I've always been a comic book buff. I've been reading them since I was 7 years old, and I've drawn a lot of inspiration from them – especially early on in my career. Comics made me want to start drawing, and although we had to draw life models in college, I think the stuff I learned on my own from tracing *Spiderman* comics gave me a better insight into human anatomy. I don't think our models would have hung upside down from a wall just so we could see how their deltoids reacted!

Dave: *Seven* came out when I was in my early twenties, and my university career was getting me down. Chalk it up to a quarter-life crisis if you like, but it's what got me into design. Instead of dating an 18-year-old and buying a 'vette, I bought myself a Mac.

Dave: Comics? I love Frank Miller's *Sin City*, and a few other comic book artists, but I get most of my inspiration from solid blocks of type. Too many years studying, analyzing, and just reading for pure enjoyment I guess.

ED: Could you say a few words about your approach to the task of remixing the others' work, and the thinking behind the pieces you eventually produced?

Brian: The idea of changing or altering the work of the other artists was difficult at first. I certainly didn't feel the need to try and improve their work in any way, or indeed that I had the right to do so. I felt that I needed to come up with some valid reason to remix the work of the others, rather than making changes just for the sake of it. I decided that it would be interesting to try to tie the works together in some way, and at the same time to fit them into the series of images comprising my own contribution.

I achieved this by using three basic design elements in each piece: the background color, the red color that I'd used in my own designs, and the typography. Trying to retain the integrity of the original pieces, while making them look like they were part of the image series in my own work, was an interesting exercise. Nathan's piece was probably the one with which I took the most liberties: I discarded all but the main abstract element. Dave's work was more or less just a case of changing the colors to the new design palette, and Tom's piece was desaturated and then filled with the red color using Screen mode.

Looking at the three images alongside my own pieces, I feel that it worked out pretty successfully, and it was an interesting way to finish the project. I'm looking forward to seeing how everything works out in print.

4x4 // COLLAB // NATHAN

4

x

4

4x4 // COLLAB // DAVE

COMPLEXITY

COMPLEXITY

COMPLEXITY

COMPLEXITY

4x4 // COLLAB // TOM

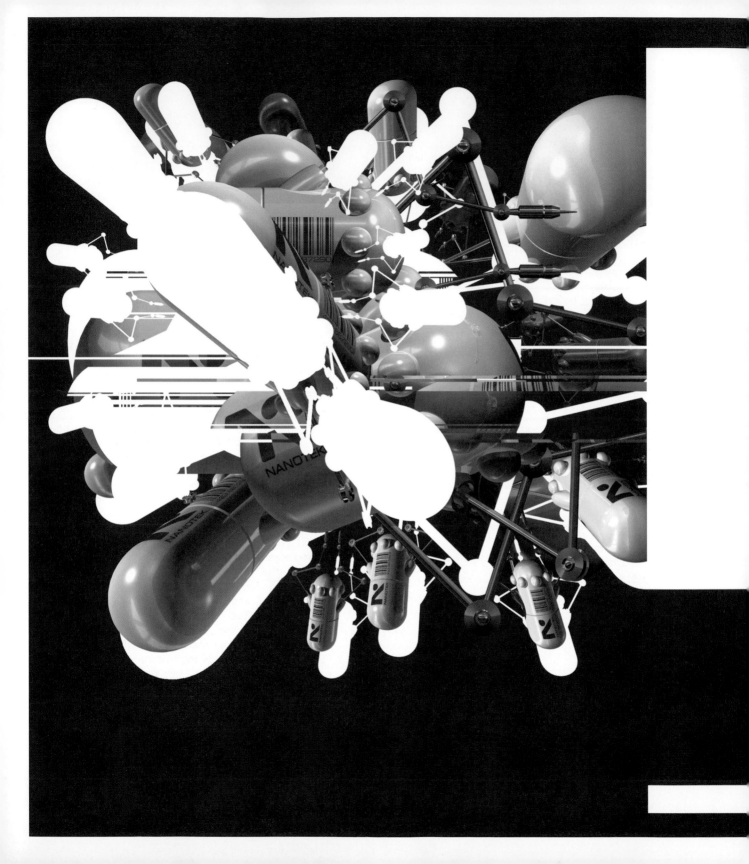

Dave: There's a certain amount of schizophrenia involved in collaborating with another artist. Or is multiple personality disorder a closer diagnosis? During the process of remixing the other three authors' works, I often had problems separating my work from theirs. In taking license with another person's work, was I simply imposing my styles and processes with the authority of an iron bar and a jackboot, or was a true collaborative spirit present as I set to work with the other authors' PSDs?

The main source of aggravation when approaching Brian's contributions was that there were so many options to choose from! The decision to use the nanobots as central design elements, though, was simply a matter of viewing all the files simultaneously, and then picking out the recurring themes. Functionally, I copied and pasted the different instances of the nanobots into a giant collage, and then set about imposing some of myself on the images. In my own contribution, I'd achieved an effect that I rather liked by obliterating the detail in an object and then leaving it as a silhouette. I approached the nanobots in the same manner, and I began to like the new shapes and patterns that emerged as a result of the interaction. This seemed in keeping with the Chaos theme, and after a little tweaking of positions here and there, I was done. It was a simple build, and I'm fairly sure that the strength of the models themselves provided the necessary motivation and inspiration.

The remix I effected on Tom's piece is the one I had most problems with. I was presented with a visually stunning work that I had only a vague idea of how to deal with. The solution to this, though, was fairly simple: I decided to take a direct and mathematical approach to the piece, and let things sort themselves out. I broke the file down into its base parts and then introduced some elements from my own work to carry the idea of collaboration further. I laid out the images as I would pictures in a gallery – in simple, progressive rows – and then overlaid some of the petal structures from my own piece. Once I had that, I started experimenting with position and size until I thought I'd achieved a sense of balance with these elements (using two pages helped me to distribute the elements more cleanly). The type I used was a mixture of my own concepts of pattern recognition, and Tom's notions of complexity. The end result is something I'm pretty satisfied with, and I like the weight that each of the elements enjoys on the page. At the same time, I hope the piece maintains a large portion of Tom's original vision.

PATTERN RECOGNITION PROTOCOLS

SIMPLICITY

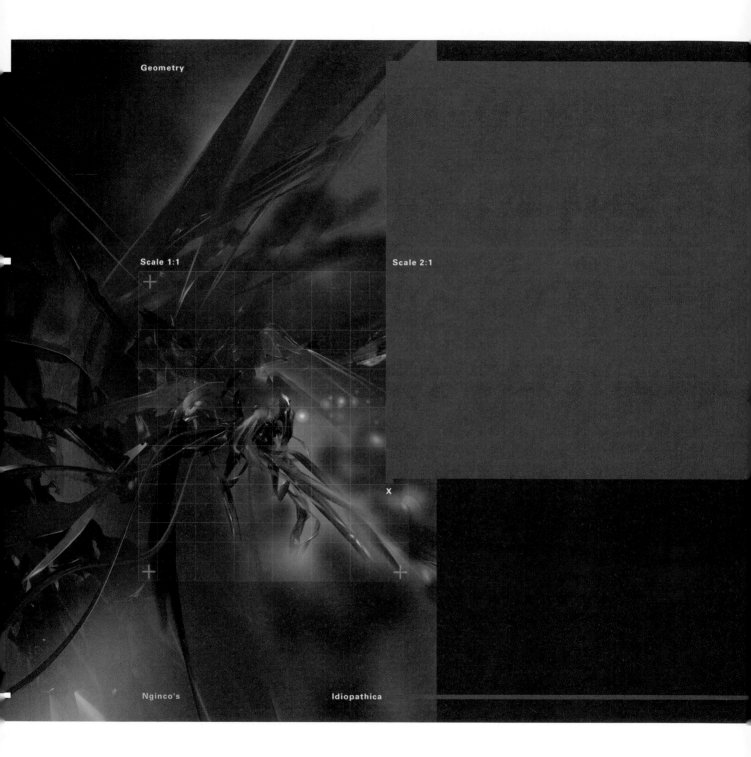

Geometry

Scale 1:1

Scale 2:1

x

Nginco's

Idiopathica

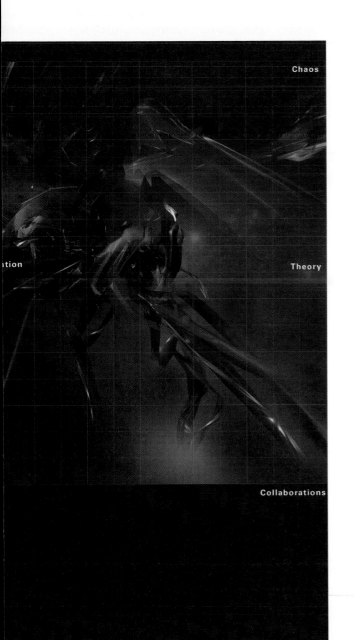

Chaos

Theory

...tion

Collaborations

vs. Deepseat.net

Nathan's submission looked like a bug to me. And in keeping with my usual textbook approach, I further decided that it was a damned good-looking bug that needed some closer examination. It was a fairly simple build, because I decided that I didn't want to exact as much change as I had with Tom and Brian's pieces. Maybe it was a carryover from Tom's piece (I created both remixes in the same session), but I was leery about doing too much with the file. My attempts to inject more of my own methods and philosophies conflicted too drastically with Nathan's piece, so I decided that a simple approach was the best thing. In the end, I chose an attractive piece of real estate and magnified it at a 2:1 scale; applying the grid gave the illusion that I had done so with some purpose. The next step was simply to choose snippets of appropriate grammar, and to apply the same kind of grid-like structure in an attempt to frame the artwork. My only complaint was that it was a pretty superficial approach to the theme, as I was just exploring different layout ideas. I was satisfied with the end result, however, and at the time I was really starting to like the two-page layout thing.

To me, collaboration has always involved a running dialog, but here we were simply given access to each others' completed PSD files and asked to make something new. This being the situation, I took each artist's work further down the path that they had begun, but I also injected a piece of myself into these new designs. There was no helping that part of the equation, really: I was a bit of a control freak, working in isolation from the other three artists. Somewhere in the creation of these pieces, I became as attached to them as I was to my original, which for me has always been the sign of a successful partnership.

Nathan: Remixing the other authors' pieces took quite a bit of thought, especially Brian's – he'd modeled objects, rather than shapes, and I was confused at first as to how I was going to use them.

Undaunted, I started off with Tom's piece, and while the process was a little slow, I actually found it the easiest to work with. I'm not sure why; it just was.

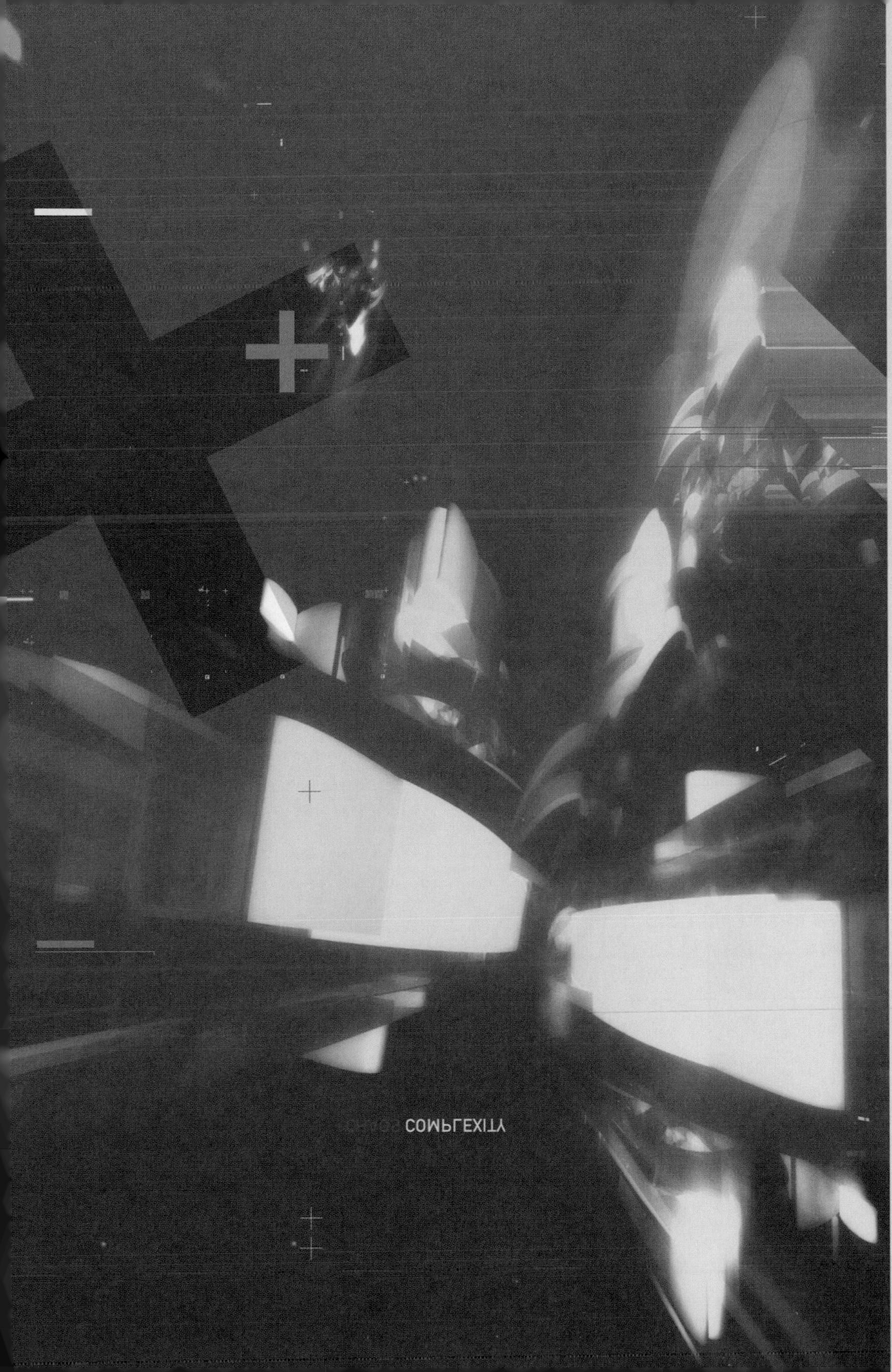
COMPLEXITY

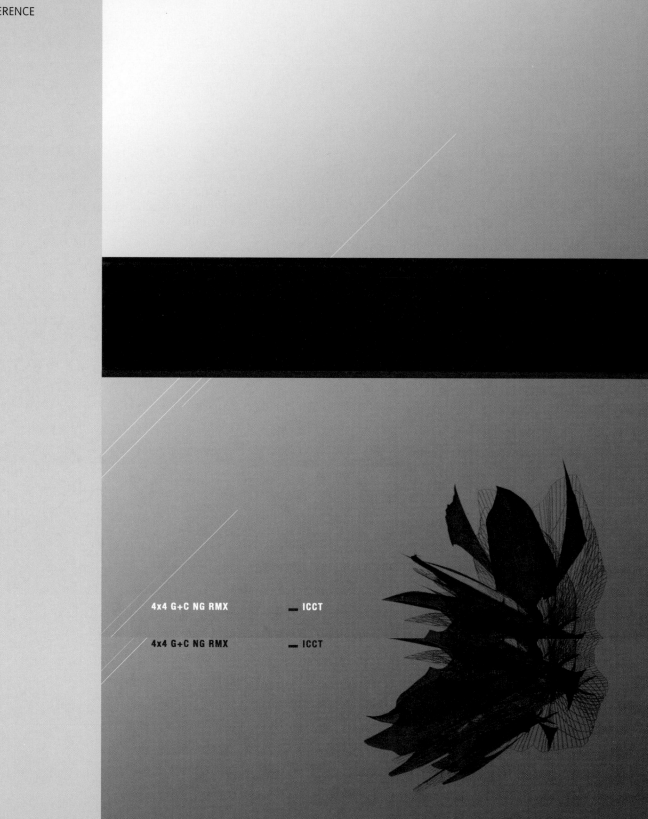

4x4 G+C NG RMX   — ICCT

4x4 G+C NG RMX   — ICCT

Next came Dave's piece, and that one really did take quite a long time. I tried a number of different approaches, but didn't really care for any of them. In the end, I went for something quite minimal.

And finally came Brian's, which had more revisions than any of the others. I tried several things, from a very abstract composition with shapes all over it, to not very much at all. At first I was using bright colors, but that wasn't getting me very far. When I darkened it up a bit, I began to feel far more comfortable. In the end, I ended up taking a lot away of what I'd added, because it looked too cluttered.

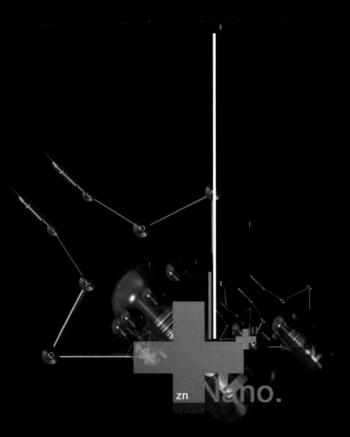

Tom: I look some time off between finishing my piece for this book and working on the remixes, and by the time I got back, I didn't have the luxury of being able to spend hours and hours on each piece. Thankfully, all the pieces were already strong, and the brief was aimed at getting a 'gut reaction', so I just went with my instincts.

I started with Nathan's image: it had a nice, abstract quality, and it gave me a good base to work from. So I did my thing: I threw some white boxes at it, and tweaked it a little (offsetting it, and desaturating it slightly). I didn't want to overdo it, though, or I'd lose the original in the stuff I just added to it – so I stopped.

Next up was Brian, who'd given me ten images to choose from! I picked the one in the bluish tone with the nanobots flying towards the viewer, and it struck me that it could be fun to combine those bots with my 3D composition, and let them fly out of that image. Instead of creating some totally new images, I just combined two existing ones – and then I threw a big white box on top, just for good measure!

With Dave's image, I had more problems. I got the feeling that his initial design lay very close to mine in terms of design: lots of white space, and colored boxes. I couldn't just do my 'white box' thing – in fact, I almost didn't want to do a remix of his image at all, because it felt too close to home. But I gave it a try anyway: I threw out almost all the layers, until I had only his initial 3D structure. I set the background color to match the one from his 3D structure, and put a big white box in between the two to separate them, and to pull the 3D in to focus. Then I threw in some extra details to flesh out/balance the composition, and I was done.

get it daily

mikecina.com
trueistrue.com
weworkforthem.com